MW00564393

FASHION PORTFOLIO

LAURENCE KING

First published in Great Britain in 2023 by

Laurence King Student & Professional
An imprint of Quercus Editions Ltd
Carmelite House
50 Victoria Embankment
London EC4Y oDZ

An Hachette UK company

Copyright © Text 2023 Tamara Albu and
Michelle Nahum-Albright

The moral right of Tamara Albu and Michelle Nahum-Albright to be
identified as the authors of this work has been asserted in accordance
with the Copyright, Designs and Patents Act, 1988.

All rights reserved. No part of this publication may be reproduced or
transmitted in any form or by any means, electronic or mechanical,
including photocopy, recording, or any information storage and
retrieval system, without permission in writing from the publisher.

A CIP catalogue record for this book is available from the
British Library

TPB ISBN 978-1-91394-792-7

Ebook ISBN 978-1-52941-987-0

Quercus Editions Ltd hereby exclude all liability to the extent
permitted by law for any errors or omissions in this book and
for any loss, damage or expense (whether direct or indirect) suffered
by a third party relying on any information contained
in this book.

10 9 8 7 6 5 4 3 2 1

Design by Lizzie Ballantyne (lizzie b design)
Cover image courtesy Ikshit Pande (see credits page)
Back cover images by Tamara Albu

Printed and bound in China by C&C Offset Printing Co., Ltd.

Papers used by Quercus are from well-managed forests
and other responsible sources.

FASHION PORTFOLIO

CREATE | CURATE | INNOVATE

Tamara Albu & Michelle Nahum-Albright

Laurence King

Contents

Foreword

When I was asked to provide a foreword for this book and give my view on what it takes to succeed in the fashion industry, I realized that the words I wrote in my 1988 fashion manifesto are as true now as they were then. As a designer you have to manifest what you stand for and always maintain that.

My form of design is conceptual. Designing a dress is not about hiding it under a mountain of zippers, frills, buttons and leather appliqués... It's about finding the dress's essence as an object. If we eliminate the superfluous, we come to the very firm conclusion that fashion must be comfortable.

- Comfortable for the body and comfortable for the mind.
- Comfortable for those who wear it and comfortable for those who see it.
- Comfortable to produce and destroy, comfortable to put together and pull apart.

Fashion has to constantly be moving forward and this implies experimenting with new shapes, applying new materials, being inventive.

It is pretentious and ridiculous to only want to design haute couture in the 21st century. It is the equivalent of publishing overly priced editions of books that only a handful of individuals can afford or converting the largest of museums into closed-door institutions.

The only thing that should never be sacrificed in the name of price is the quality of materials. To choose acrylics over natural silks, cottons and linens is a blow to one's quality of life. It is therefore preferable to possess fewer items but of superior quality.

Designing clothes should never be just about business or industry. Designing clothes is the ultimate form of expression.

You must have the courage to embrace your own unique sense of style without ever letting yourself be intimidated by the fear of your own body or succumbing to the pressures of differentiating oneself from other prevailing aesthetics.

Agatha Ruiz de la Prada
(Text adapted from *La Moda CóModa* – 1988)

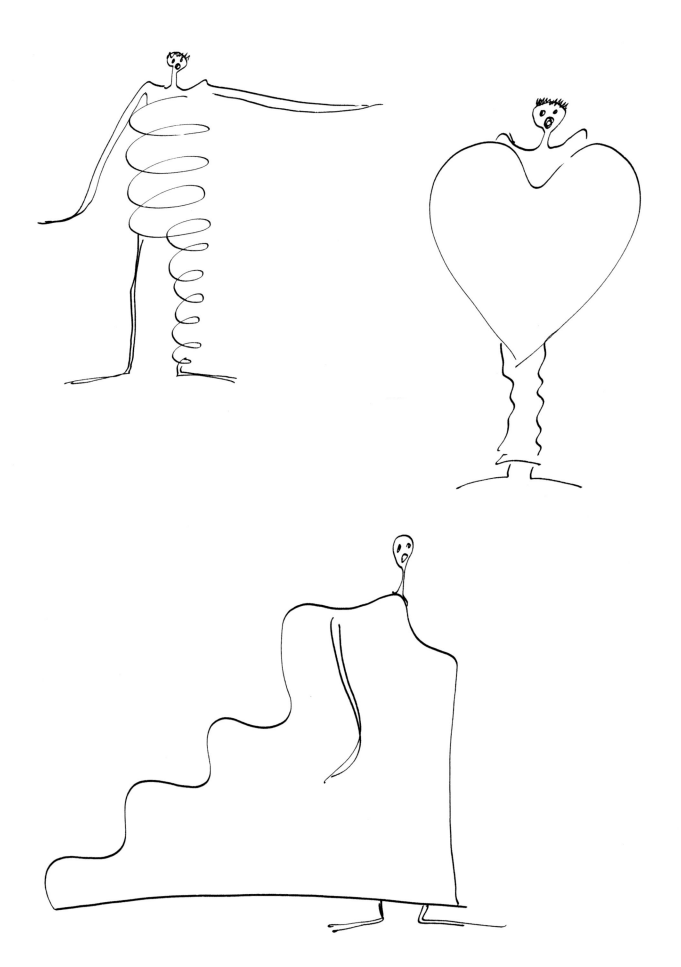

Introduction

Fashion Portfolio: Design, Curate, Innovate offers emerging fashion professionals a broad perspective on the process of presenting oneself and one's design work. Supported by abundant visual examples, each chapter is a progression of step-by-step guidance outlining distinctive aspects of strategic career positioning. Portfolio is an essential component of this wide yet personal strategy. A clear identity and the right branding places job applicants or aspiring entrepreneurs on the path to success in the rapidly evolving global fashion industry. The chapters in this book cover the full scope: collection positioning, collection development, design concept, and portfolio content to presentation. In looking at career direction and interview skills, we discuss personal branding as well as the important role of social media in self-promotion.

Chapter 1 is devoted to design development, and begins by discussing the targeted customer who is the backbone of any successful collection. Designers need to understand who they are designing for before they immerse themselves in the creative process. This same target customer and relevant market remains front and center in designing and curating a portfolio. After covering a variety of customer profiles and market perspectives, the first chapter explores the structure of collection development with an emphasis on a personal point of view. An umbrella concept may guide an entire fashion portfolio. This may include mood/inspiration boards, fabric and trimming presentations, design illustrations, technical sketches, and finished garment photography. These elements document the entire process for the viewer.

Chapter 2 highlights a designer's specific skills and the conceptual creativity that will be a hallmark of their portfolio. A wide array of fashion illustration and rendering techniques are included. This is also where the development of a sequence of strong, curated units is covered. These become the basic building blocks of a portfolio.

Chapter 3 focuses on portfolio styles, from analog to digital formats. In this third chapter, layout and aesthetics are discussed as tools to reveal the essence of the designer and make a personal statement. Designers can communicate clearly through the skillful use of composition and layout. The portfolio is presented as a visually rich enticement as well as a strong marketing tool for sharing the designer's unique energy.

Chapter 4 is dedicated to branding consistency as a method for reinforcing an individual personal statement and values. We examine graphic design choices, from logo, type, and color to photographic styling. The alignment of the résumé, business card, stationery, social media, and personal brand website becomes an integrated story. Visually and conceptually, together they create a strong singular message.

Chapter 5 addresses the overall importance of social media. We look at major media channels and their best uses. Print and video work with social media to build and reinforce a personal fashion statement.

Chapter 6 is dedicated to career categories and job search specifics. We discuss the organization for searching, effective interview preparation, one-to-one interview interaction, as well as follow-up, covering the wide scope of design opportunities in the fashion field. In addition to distinct garment design categories, we address the related fields of accessories, textiles, and theatrical costumes. As fashion and the consumer continue to develop and redefine themselves, career paths must continue to expand. We examine fashion paths that may overlap with those of a designer and offer alternative creative routes including stylist, photographer, journalist, buyer, merchandiser, archivist, and trend analyst.

We conclude our book with a selection of case studies. These profile diverse fashion designers from an assortment of cultures and countries as they launch their careers, set up their own brands, or work for established fashion houses. The struggles, strategies, and successes embedded in each personal story are both inspiring and instructive, their achievements celebrating individual paths to success. In fact, every aspect of this book integrates unique strategy as the foundation for a strong identity.

CHAPTER 1

The Collection

Defining Your Audience
Creative Process
Style, Voice, and Identity

This chapter establishes your design work as central to your portfolio and strategic personal positioning. Cohesive collections build portfolio narrative. A clear portfolio statement originates in a detailed visualization of your audience, a structured, disciplined approach to creative process, and the manifestation of a unique personal design vision.

Your portfolio needs to speak in a clear voice to emphasize skill, style, and attitude as well as establish your unique story of assets and talents. It is this voice and story, forged during your design work, that is the basis for your identity and signature style, demonstrating your ability to contribute long term. Every mood board, swatch board, set of croquis, and photograph tells the viewer who you are and why they should hire you.

Your portfolio should utilize both images and textures, the digital and physical, to showcase your competencies and capabilities. While making a strong case for a distinctive creative point of view, a well-designed portfolio also needs to demonstrate a rich awareness of the industry. In a world in transition, we cannot plan for a future; but we can prepare for the future. Always remain aware and flexible.

Defining Your Audience

A first step toward defining your signature style is asking yourself where you will place yourself in the evolving world of fashion. What kind of company do you wish to work with? Who is the consumer you want to design for? What do they value? What do *you* value? There is no substitute for researching and understanding your targets and for defining your audience.

Whether you want to be a designer with your own business or a designer working for a corporate organization, your collections need to speak the language of your clients. Developing a clear understanding of market targets allows you to see how these relate to your own skill set and strengths. Consider which market segment interests you. Is it menswear, womenswear, or perhaps bridal? The deeper your knowledge of the target market and audience, the easier it will be to position your work.

(below) Katrin Schnabl, Phenyla collection.

Customer profile

A well-defined customer profile gives voice to a portfolio. To effectively present yourself, you must create based on a distinct image of your customer.

Having a clear understanding of the customer and their specific needs and desires is crucial to the success of your collection. Establishing customer demographics—gender identification, age bracket, general lifestyle, spending behavior, cultural and social affinities, and occupation—needs to happen early in the process of collection development.

To guide the creative process, you must envision your prototype consumer. For example, a busy urban professional functioning in the constant stress and bustle of the city will make different choices to a customer with a casual lifestyle living in a country environment. A clear vision of customer demographics influences everything from silhouette and structure to fabric choice and embellishments.

In order to provide a properly targeted base for your designs, use a template to build your customer profile, with detailed information on attributes and descriptors (see over the page). The final customer portrait normally includes age group, gender identification, lifestyle, occupation, income, sales category, distribution, market, and competition, but may be expanded as necessary.

Customer Profile 1

Age	Children	Adolescent	Young Adult	Middle Age	Mature Adult			
Gender	**Female**	Male	Non-binary	Transgender				
Location	Continent i.o. Europe, Africa, Asia, North America, South America	Country	Large metropolitan area	Midsize city	Suburban	Rural		
Lifestyle	Student	Young Professional	**Established Professional**	Social Icon/Philanthropist	Self-employed	Family Caregiver		
Occupation	Technology	Finance	**Arts/Design**	Education	Sports	Entertainment	e-Commerce	Health/Science
Income Bracket	Lower	Middle	**Upper**	Higher	Alternative			
US—income	Below 19,999 USD	Between 19,999 and 164,999 USD	Between 164,999 and 249,999 USD	Above 249,999 USD	Partner earnings, trust funds, inheritance, awards			
UK—income	Below 13,900 GBP	Between 13,900 and 54,900 GBP	Between 54,900 and 175,000 GBP	Above 175,000 GBP	Partner earnings, trust funds, inheritance, awards			
Sales Category	Low/Mass	Mass	Bridge	Designer	Couture/Luxury	Niche		
Retail Price Point	$ Tens	$$ Below and above $100	$$$ Below and above $1000	$$$$ Thousands	$$$$$ Tens of thousands/ hundreds of thousands	Variable price point		
Shopping Environment	Department stores	Boutique/ specialty stores	Concept store	Designer store	Specialty store	Dedicated website	Alternate distribution	
Targeted Market	Sportswear/ Casual	Eveningwear/ Formal	Business/ Daytime formal	High-end casual wear/ Resort	High-end formal wear, day and evening	Activewear	Loungewear/ Intimate apparel/ Sleepwear/ Beachwear & Swimwear	Bridalwear/ Red carpet/ Special events
Competition Examples	Uniqlo Gap H&M Zara Mango Forever 21 Charlotte Russe Hamnett London Primark River Island	Banana Republic J. Crew Patagonia Isabelle Fox UK	Reiss Whistles Jaeger Ted Baker Cos Eileen Fisher DKNY CK Ellen Tracy	Anna Sui Phoebe Philo Matteau Resort Donna Karan Calvin Klein Stella McCartney Tom Ford Elie Tahari Gucci	Karl Lagerfeld Issey Miyake Yoji Yamamoto Saint Laurent Iris Van Herpen Dries Van Noten Christian Lacroix Vivienne Westwood Rêve En Vert	Nike Adidas Puma Reebok Under Armour	Gottex Matteau Swim Heidi Klein Nautica Natori Anne Cole	Vera Wang Oscar de la Renta Christina Wu Marchesa Bridal Naeem Khan Jenny Packham Reem Acra Nicole Lan Yu

This targeted customer is someone in their mid-thirties. The designer envisions the customer as intellectual and artistic. She may have studied art history and become an art dealer, working at a prestigious gallery. A hectic daily schedule may involve auctions and clients. Our purchaser lives and works in the city, enjoying its spirit and activity. A very active social life takes her to exhibitions, show openings, and concerts. There is satisfaction in being noticed in the crowd. Substantial income allows designer choices. For daytime, she tends to choose Calvin Klein, Marc Jacobs, Maison Margiela, Issey Miyake, or Yoji Yamamoto.

Customer Profile 2

Age	Children	Adolescent	Young Adult	**Middle Age**	Mature Adult			
Gender	**Female**	Male	Non-binary	Transgender				
Location	Continent i.e. Europe, Africa, Asia, North America, South America	Country	Large metropolitan area	Midsize city	**Suburban**	Rural		
Lifestyle	Student	Young Professional	**Established Professional**	Social Icon/ Philanthropist	Self-employed	Family Caregiver		
Occupation	Technology	Finance	Arts/Design	Education	Sports	Entertainment	e-Commerce	**Health/Science**
Income Bracket	Lower	**Middle**	Upper	Higher	Alternative			
US—income	Below 19,999 USD	Between 19,999 and 164,999 USD	Between 164,999 and 249,999 USD	Above 249,999 USD	Partner earnings, trust funds, inheritance, awards			
UK—income	Below 13,900 GBP	Between 13,900 and 54,900 GBP	Between 54,900 and 175,000 GBP	Above 175,000 GBP	Partner earnings, trust funds, inheritance, awards			
Sales Category	Low/Mass	Mass	**Bridge**	Designer	Couture/Luxury	Niche		
Retail Price Point	$ Tens	$$ Below and above $100	**$$$ Below and above $1000**	$$$$ Thousands	$$$$$ Tens of thousands/ hundreds of thousands	Variable price point		
Shopping Environment	Department stores	Boutique/ Specialty stores	Concept store	Designer store	Specialty store	Dedicated website	Alternate distribution	
Targeted Market	Sportswear/ Casual	Eveningwear/ Formal	Business/ Daytime formal	High-end casual wear/ Resort	High-end formal wear, day and evening	Activewear	Loungewear/ Intimate apparel/ Sleepwear/ Beachwear & Swimwear	Bridalwear/ Red carpet/ Special events
Competition Examples	Uniqlo Gap H&M Zara Mango Forever 21 Charlotte Russe Hamnett London Primark River Island	Banana Republic J. Crew **Patagonia** **Isabelle Fox UK**	Reiss Whistles Jaeger **Ted Baker** Cos Eileen Fisher DKNY CK Ellen Tracy	Anna Sui Phoebe Philo Matteau Resort Donna Karan Calvin Klein Stella McCartney Tom Ford Elie Tahari Gucci	Karl Lagerfeld Issey Miyake Yoji Yamamoto Saint Laurent Iris Van Herpen Dries Van Noten Christian Lacroix Vivienne Westwood, Rêve En Vert	Nike Adidas Puma Reebok Under Armour	Gottex Matteau Swim Heidi Klein Nautica Natori Anne Cole	Vera Wang Oscar de la Renta Christina Wu Marchesa Bridal Naeem Khan Jenny Packham Reem Acra Nicole Lan Yu

This customer is a young, professional woman living in the suburbs of a large or midsize city. With a scientific background, she may be an environmental scientist, biochemist, or some type of scientific researcher.

She and her partner share an upper middle-class lifestyle. They enjoy nature. Her spare time is filled with gardening, hiking, and traveling to exotic, pristine places. Leisure clothing is usually selected from Patagonia and Isabelle Fox (UK). This customer is practical and logical. In clothing, she craves comfort and long-lasting quality. Environmentally sensitive, she is always looking for ethical fashion labels. When choosing something new, she searches for up-and-coming designers who share her sustainable values.

Some designers choose to model a customer profile based on themselves. Even in this case, when the designer personally understands all the aspects needed to define the image and assumes a customer base with similar taste to their own, a structured profile analysis can benefit the final collection— and portfolio.

(above left and right) Eileen Fisher collections are inspired by her own minimalistic and timeless style.

(above) In 2019, at 97, the American businesswoman, interior designer, and style icon Iris Apfel signed a modeling contract with global agency IMG.

Gender

Each collection you design must clearly define a gender or take a non-gendered approach to the targeted customer. From a business perspective, it is essential for the buyers, clientele, media, and the consumer to fully understand the collection category and gender sales target. This helps define retail positioning. Traditional menswear and womenswear are being joined by an increasing number of gender fluid clothing lines.

Age bracket

Customarily, age bracket is important in developing a focused collection. However, age itself is less important than understanding the lifestyle it indicates. Understanding a teenager's lifestyle will help keep a junior collection contemporary. Filled with a unique set of needs and desires, the life of a professional in their twenties or thirties will reflect an alternate culture. For these professionals, a morning meeting could require formal office attire. A cocktail party later in the day could mean a total change of clothing or a quick restyling.

There is increased flexibility within fashion. It celebrates style across all ages. Activity, lifestyle, and personal preference are defining factors. More than ever, the consumer defines the direction of fashion.

(left) Stella Shared by Stella McCartney is a unisex capsule collection for a rising cohort finding their voices. They leverage self-expression to bring positive social change to the world. The campaign includes a cohort of next-gen Chinese creators led by actor Leo Wu.

Spending behavior

As market and retail conditions continue to change, spending behavior remains directly connected to collection price point. A high-profile entertainer could present themselves in haute couture garments, selecting items for image impact, projection of status, or craftsmanship. A young professional is likely to buy designer or bridge outfits, selecting for cost and functionality in addition to look. Out of necessity, a college student or young adult living on a fixed budget is more likely to choose mass-market. See Market Segmentation, p.18.

Cultural and social affinities

The activities an individual enjoys will often influence purchase choices. For travelers, mix-and-match separates, multifunctional garments, and easy-care fabrication may be preferred. Those with an outdoor or sports orientation need specific comfortable garments and footwear for rugged environments. Philanthropic functions or black-tie receptions often require the more formal evening gown and tuxedo. Attire may be designer couture, prêt-à-porter, or more widely distributed brands.

Occupation and professional life

The tech sector has had significant influence on professional uniforms. Someone working in the same occupation may choose to dress formally or casually based on the culture of the company they work for. For instance, working in a start-up company, a hoodie with chinos will often be acceptable. Even in the finance sector the Monday-through-Thursday conservative suit is replaced with a more relaxed look for "casual Friday". An art gallery curator may choose an unconventional or eclectic look, unlike someone working in banking, whose employer may require a conservative suit. For creative fields the dress code is often more fluid. As remote working becomes more standard, consumer clothing needs to continue to evolve. Fashion opportunity grows as environments change and acceptable choices multiply.

Sustainable and ethical values

Many customers share the values of designers who are responsible in their practices. They will seek out designers that create less waste and less environmental damage and use labor in a more ethical way, examining material selection closely for a biodegradable choice. Clothing designed to have a second life may be favored.

(below) Comfortable, versatile garments that allow freedom of movement go from gym to streetwear.

(right) Allbirds believes in the power of natural materials and their potential to transform ecosystems. Nature is their muse.

Market segmentation

There are various interpretations of price point segmentation. Price points shift as markets and consumers realign in our evolving world. As customer needs and desires evolve, the definition of price point segmentation has become less strictly defined, with some blurring between the categories.

For the sake of clarity, this book organizes womenswear markets with price points into three major sectors: high-end luxury market, intermediate mass-market, and low-end mass-market. Each one contains several subdivisions.

PRICE POINT MARKET SEGMENTATION

HIGH-END LUXURY MARKET

Haute Couture

Couture

Designer | Prêt-à-porter (Transitional)

INTERMEDIATE MASS-MARKET

Diffusion (Secondary Line)

Bridge (Transitional and/or Secondary)

Better (Transitional and/or Secondary)

Contemporary (Secondary Line)

LOW-END MASS MARKET

Moderate

Budget and Discount

HIGH-END LUXURY MARKET

Average garment cost: $$$$-$$$$$

Catering to the higher end of the market, including superior quality materials and finishing.

Haute couture is the highest and most exclusive segment. Focused on singular designs, this highly protected category includes only fashion houses meeting the strict standards of the Chambre Syndicale de la Haute Couture (CSHC). Haute couture caters to preeminent figures who pay for the artistry, skill, and status of this designation. This is the most limited production tier, featuring hand stitching as well as labor-intensive detailing and finishing. It is produced by a team of highly skilled technicians and unique artisans in the designer's atelier or associated specialty workshops. Examples of these designers include: Jean Paul Gaultier, Christian Dior, and Viktor & Rolf.

(opposite) Viktor & Rolf, Haute Couture F/W 2016.
(below) Iris van Herpen, Couture S/S 2020.

(below) Vivienne Westwood, RTW Fall 2020.

Couture is sometimes used as a transitional market classification between the haute couture and designer segments. Haute couture and couture share several characteristics. They both create *made-to-measure* or *made-to-order* garments and require multiple customer fittings. Created from the highest quality materials, they are both labor intensive and primarily hand sewn. While not meeting CSHC restrictions, the outstanding designers within the couture classification still earn well-deserved recognition for their unique talent and creativity. Examples of these designers include: Alexander McQueen (McQueen himself designed for the haute couture house Givenchy), as well as Iris van Herpen and Balenciaga, guest and former members of the CSHC respectively.

The **designer** segment first emerged in Italy to meet an increasing demand for more affordable well-made garments of fine design. Lowering the price point from couture to *prêt-à-porter* (literally "ready-to-wear") was possible due to the industrialization of production. A wide range of sizes and colorways are generated within the same style. Although the labor and materials are still of very high quality, increased production causes a significant drop in cost per garment. Examples include: Vivienne Westwood, Tom Ford, Gucci, and Prada. This category also includes products produced by large multinational corporations such as LVMH.

INTERMEDIATE MASS-MARKET

Average garment cost: $$$-$$$$

The intermediate market includes mainstream brands that have further lowered merchandise cost by increasing the quantity of pieces per style produced. They offer a wider range of sizes and colorways, incorporating less expensive textiles and embellishments than in the designer segment, thus the merchandise becomes more accessible and distribution wider. This category includes several price points targeted for a variety of customers.

Diffusion is a marketing strategy that allows luxury and intermediate segments to diversify and expand the range of their targeted customers without diluting the original base. Examples of diffusion ranges and their parent labels include: Versus for Versace, DKNY for Donna Karan, and Marc for Marc Jacobs.

Bridge has its roots in the American fashion industry. It is positioned as a transitional segment between designer and the larger mass-market segment. It is the result of department store demand for good quality product at an even lower price, and the need to diversify business models to capture additional clients in an increasingly competitive market. Licensed goods and expanded market segments profitably support the high-end collections and the overall brand. Examples include: Emporio Armani, Ralph by Ralph Lauren, and Kors of Michael Kors.

Better is a less well-defined transitional segment, usually situated between bridge and contemporary. It has similar product and marketing characteristics to bridge but is offered at a slightly lower price. Department stores such as Harrods, Selfridges, and Nordstrom stock this segment. Examples include: Sandro, Stefanel, and Hobbs.

Contemporary features similar prices to the better category but often targets a younger customer. Both fashion houses and retailer private label offer product within this category. Examples include: Ted Baker, COS designs, and private label brands such as Nordstrom's Zella.

(below) COS, LFW September 2021.

LOW-END MASS-MARKET

Average garment $$-$$$

Most widely affordable category for the broadest number of consumers.

(above) H&M, RTW S/S 2018.

Mass-market aims to provide merchandise for the widest range of fashion-conscious consumers. The segment offers affordability, immediacy, and versatility, but with lower quality fabrication and labor. A seductive purchase environment is created by offering the latest fashion trends in multiple seasonal deliveries. Examples of worldwide mass-market chain retailers include H&M and Uniqlo.

High meets low This segment pioneered the collaborations, which benefit both the high- and low-end brands involved by expanding their markets and building name recognition. Collaborations have resulted in extraordinary sales jumps. Examples of "high-meets-low" collaborations include: Karl Lagerfeld and Sonia Rykiel for H&M, and Stella McCartney for H&M and Gap.

Inclusive The democratization of fashion has led designers to create collections affordable "to all, anytime, anywhere". Body-positive retailer Universal Standard calls this "Fashion Freedom for All".

Moderate fits into this wide distribution low-end segment, just above the lowest priced brands. Examples include: Nine West, Levi's, and Gap.

Budget and discount aims to provide the very lowest price. To hit the mark, production cuts corners, using inexpensive materials with poor finishing, cheap labor, and large-scale production. Unsold product from other categories is redistributed at a reduced price in discount outlets. Those who develop goods for this segment primarily "adapt" higher priced styles or, like Target, utilize designers to create affordable lines exclusively for them. Examples include: Isaac Mizrahi, Cynthia Rowley, and Todd Oldham for Target.

Customer story

Once you have a good understanding of market segmentation, look at focusing your vision. You must create both a broad and a detailed ideal customer description. Once you have analyzed age group and gender identification, drill down to more specifics. How does your target customer function in the world? What are their interests? What do they require in a wardrobe? Is their business life casual or formal? What brands currently serve their needs? Is something they need or want notably missing?

Choose a few adjectives to describe your customers. These will serve as an easy shorthand. Refer back to them during the design process. Lifestyle details tell a large part of the customer story. Occupation and background offer fascinating information about disposable income and spending habits. As you plan, remember collection price points connect directly to a customer's social and financial position. Learn all you can.

Creative Process

The creative process is complex and non-linear. Experimenting is part of the protocol, and leads to exciting discovery. It demands an abundance of imagination and passion. The process of designing fashion does not have a well-defined beginning and end. It cannot be tied to a 9-to-5 schedule. Inspiration may visit randomly. Taking a walk or listening to a song can spark an idea. These inspirations percolate and emerge in their own time; a ride on the subway, daydreaming, or sleeping may bring forth exciting possibilities.

Inspiration

A designer can draw inspiration from anything: a time period, a manner of material manipulation, or a specific muse. When this inspiration is clearly demonstrated within your portfolio, it informs and supports the customer profile. Inspiration is part of the unique story of your collection. It sets you apart and calls to employers. Some designers are inspired by an actual person, their image or style. This could be an iconic figure such as Princess Diana, or a pop icon such as Prince. Others find outsiders such as Teddy Boys or Punks motivating. In some cases designers tap into their own needs, desires, shopping habits, aesthetic affinities, or socio-economic background to model collections for audiences like themselves. In these cases, the designer acts as their own target customer, or even as their own muse.

(opposite) Karl Lagerfeld sketching.

(below) Yves Saint Laurent sketch with swatch and notes, and the finished garment.

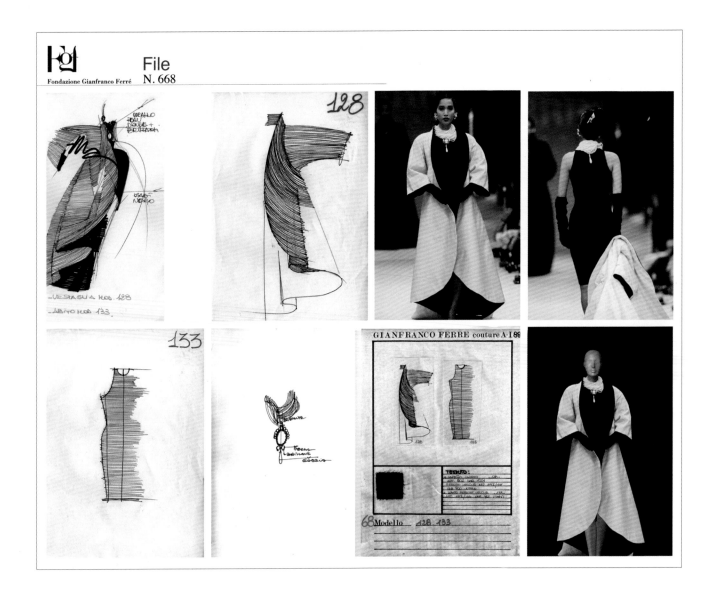

The sketchbook as a designer's diary

Interesting designs may come to you in the blink of
an eye. To avoid losing them, it is essential to develop
a system to capture your ideas while they are fresh.
Every designer finds their own method of collecting
thoughts. Some prefer a sketchbook, others use
dedicated folders organized by category: for example
sketches and notes, research and inspirational
images, and fabric sourcing. These are all forms of a
designer's diary or journal and offer a refuge for you
to create and experiment without any self-imposed
restrictions. The unleashed imagination results in a
flood of ideas to be curated and culled later. Sketches
are usually rough and filled with creative immediacy.
They can be supported by quick notes, fabric
swatches, and bits of reference. A diary may serve
as a way to document or plan a fashion show.

(above) Gianfranco Ferré, gala evening coat in velvet and *peau
d'ange* color taffeta. F/W 1988–89 couture collection design specs.

(opposite, left and right) Anna Sui, S/S 2007 collection. Sketch and
garment of Pirate Dress inspired by Marie Antoinette, pirates, and
rock 'n' roll.

This intimate personal collection may supply material
for a mood board. Waiting within this barrage of
creative thought may be a collection concept, theme,
silhouette information, a color story or fabric story.
We all have good days, when ideas pour out, and
those other days when nothing seems to work.
A journal's treasures can pay off when you confront
these dry periods.

Collection units

A fashion collection contains several modules, often referred to as "units". Each unit is based on a specific color theme called a "color story" or "color palette". It includes a fabric story, textures, details, and silhouettes. The units are broadly connected to each other through the master collection concept.

The average amount of units in a portfolio is 3–5. Consider what best represents you. Examine your designs carefully and use them deliberately to focus on your personal perspective. As you question your work, list your discoveries in a concise format. These significant attributes will help guide you in creating a brief yet comprehensive designer statement that will be evident in your portfolio.

Unit concept expressed in a distinctive name	BLOCK 1 Unit Title	
Brief written statement of unit idea	BLOCK 2 Concept Statement	
Key inspiration images supporting unit concept: fabric, color, texture stories, and silhouettes/construction details on individual boards	BLOCK 3 Mood Board	Inspiration Theme Texture Color Palette
Swatches of physical materials and trimmings	BLOCK 4 Swatches	
Photographic documentation: design process, sourcing, draping, patternmaking, and fitting	BLOCK 5 Design Process	
Finalized design sketches	BLOCK 6 Renderings	
Precise line technical drawings: detailing design details, construction lines, stitches, and seams	BLOCK 7 Flat Sketches	
Final prototype photographs: models in settings, styled with accessories, makeup, and hair	BLOCK 8 Finished Garments	

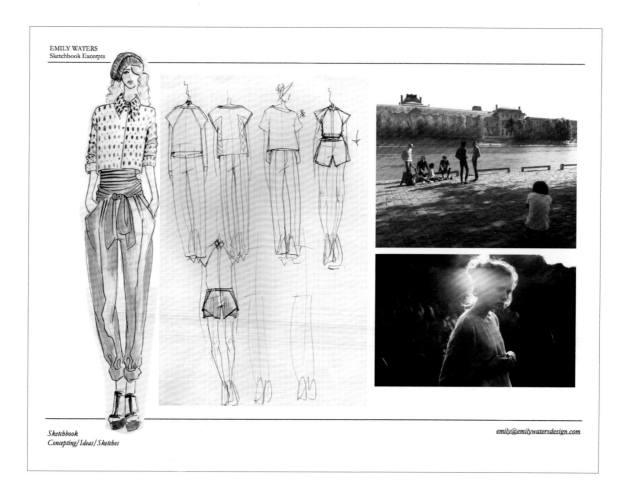

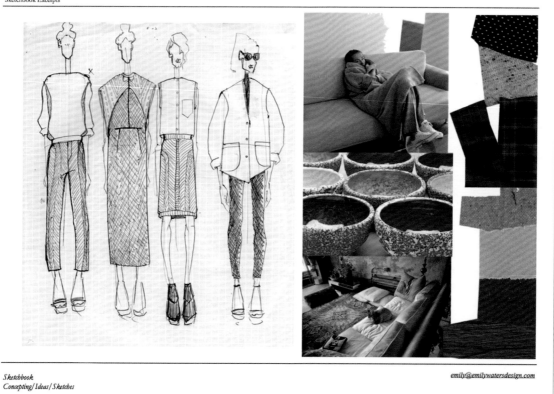

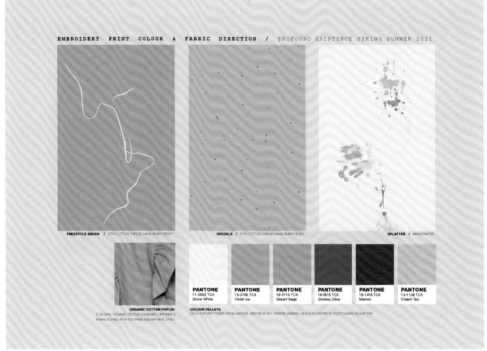

(opposite) Emily Waters Lee, sketchbook, research process, fabric and color story.

(above) Mayuri Sarof, Profound Existence S/S 2021 collection. Mood board, color and fabric story, and rendered sketches of selected designs.

The mood board

The mood board communicates the essence of a collection at a glance. It is usually included with every unit. In the portfolio the mood board may either precede garment images or act as a backdrop. The mood board is integral and incorporates visual elements supporting the collection concept. It includes theme colors, textures, and shapes. It should always include a collection title, and a concept paragraph may be added to deepen viewer understanding within a collection.

(left and below) Céline Haddad, mood board and swatch board.

(opposite, anti-clockwise) Lishuang Xu, Wabi Sabi collection: mood boards; color and texture representation; material experimentation; final garment.

The fabrics are created by re-grouping rough selvedges.

Among the five elements of Chinese philosophy,
gold (metal) stands for the state of declining I created some fabrics by combining metal and cloth.

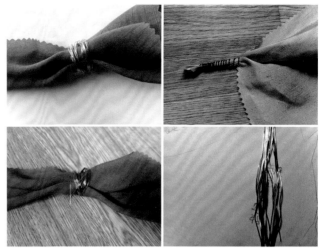

Color story and swatch board

The color story and/or swatch board follow the mood board. This information relating to color may be introduced either before or with garment images. A color selection may originate from a standardized color reference table, such as Pantone Color Matching System, or from one of the trend services such as WGSN, Peclers Paris, or Trend Union. Based on personal research, you will configure several sets of color palettes for each season. Each color palette is a core element of a collection unit. Fabric selection always follows these established color palettes. Depending on the price point, the textile mill may customize or develop fabrics exclusively for a designer collection. Consider including optional garment-construction process photographs.

Photography

Experimenting and developing variations on your chosen theme is essential to collection creativity. Documenting these experiments by photographing them is always a good practice. Not all variations will translate into finished garments, but showing selected process material in your portfolio in addition to finished garments is essential for demonstrating to a potential employer a marriage of creative and technical skills.

(above) Carla Amaning A. Kwarteng, collection unit, mood and swatch boards.

(opposite) Amina Lyazidi, mood boards.

- ARCHITECTURE
- FUR
- VOLUME
- SQUARE

THEME

- AUTUMN / SEPIA COLORS

FW2014

Croquis

The quick sketches done during a fashion show or a creative meeting are called croquis or "fashion poses". They usually become part of the designer's sketchbook and may be rough or rendered. From this initial stage of random sketches, designers move on to refining the designs. As your collection concept begins to take shape, there will be various iterations as you work toward a cohesive version of your vision.

At this later stage, rendered sketches are developed depicting additional design details and following a more precise color palette, silhouette, texture, and style quality. Physical construction may be limited by cost, material, or time constraints. Rendered sketches of an entire collection become a way to demonstrate your creativity and originality, free of these burdens.

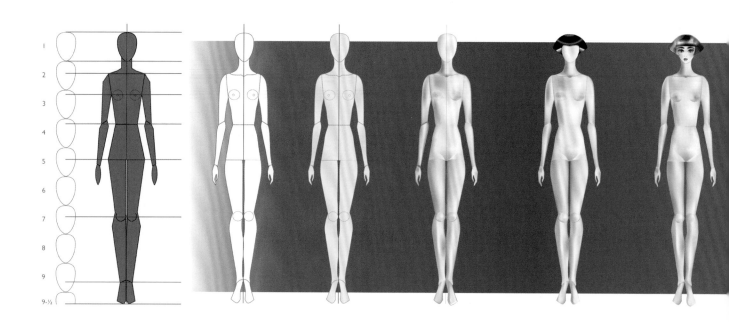

Straight pose development is a support for garment silhouette, proportion, and design elements. Body movement and head features are omitted to allow full focus on the geometry of a garment. A stronger focus on the garment may be achieved by eliminating facial features and hair. A slight alteration of the straight pose can call attention to specific garment details. One of the arms is bent to reach the side pocket in the second illustration, otherwise this important construction detail would not be noticed.

(opposite) Tamara Albu, Illustrator renderings: straight pose steps and four color-blocked garments.

(below) Tamara Albu, Illustrator renderings: five action poses and poses demonstrating fabric, texture, and weight in relation to a garment. Three garments are shown, representing various textures of lightweight fabric.

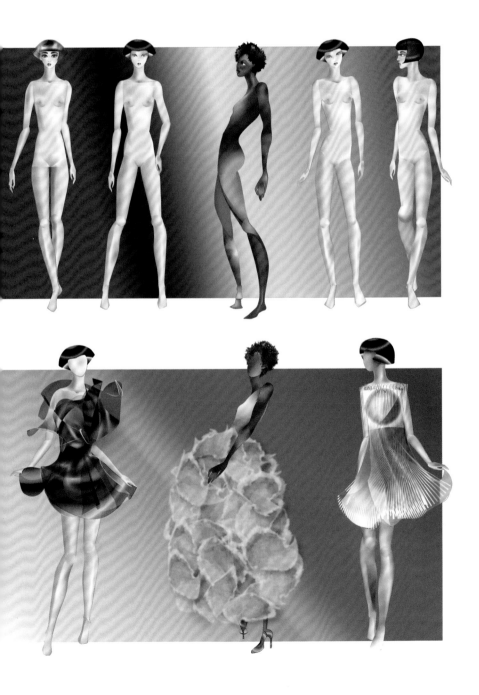

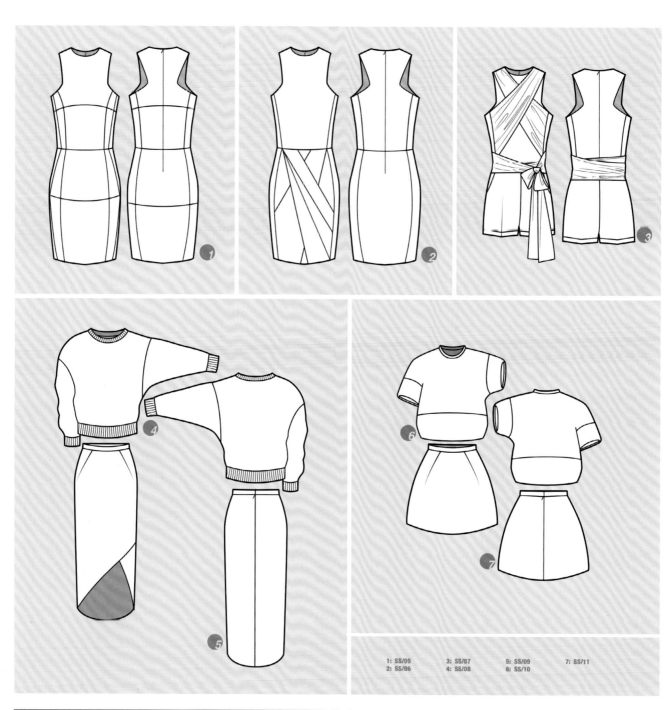

1: SS/05	3: SS/07	5: SS/09	7: SS/11
2: SS/06	4: SS/08	6: SS/10	

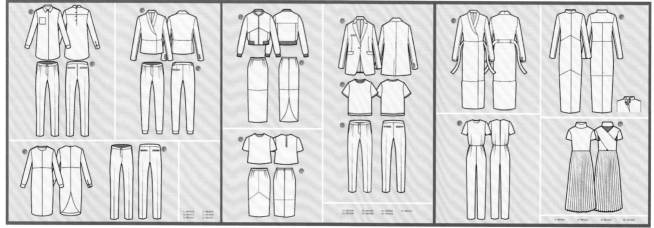

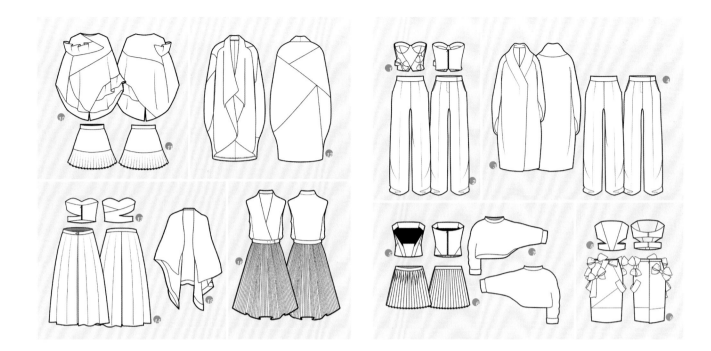

(opposite, top) Mayuri Sarof, Urban Story collection, flat sketches.

(opposite, below) Mayuri Sarof, Escape collection, flat sketches.

(above, left and right) Mayuri Sarof, Shadows collection, flat sketches.

Technical sketches/flats

A portfolio without technical sketches loses credibility. For an employer, flats demonstrate that you have immediately usable practical skills. Within a portfolio, full measurements and specifications are not required if the flats accompany rendered sketches. Flats rendered in black and white may be presented with corresponding garment designs or gathered together into a flats page. You could decide to eliminate all rendered croquis, presenting the collection only as full-color detailed rendered flats.

Moving your vision forward

Allow specific themes, color and fabric stories, textures, and silhouettes to become organizing principles of your collection. Create consistency throughout your collection, but avoid using the same defining factors for each unit and make sure to build in unexpected elements. For instance, Giorgio Armani's favorite color palettes are usually monochromatic. Although neutral colors may be predominant in the brand's collections, the themes, details, silhouettes, and textures within each collection will not repeat themselves from unit to unit—instead, the use of neutrals will be the link between the units. Consider each unit as a set of essential components and add a group of variable parts. The unit should incorporate a mood board and a fabric/swatch board as well as the rendered sketches of a specific theme. It can also include flat sketches, development process photographs, and photographs of finished garments.

Let's examine Agatha Ruiz de la Prada S/S 2018 collection to identify the characteristics that make it unique and recognizable. Happiness spills from the designs of Agatha Ruiz de la Prada; bright color sings, and her simple silhouettes are filled with joyful play. Color blocking, geometric shapes and patterns, child-like drawings, and short text in naïve fonts create an unmistakable signature look. Abstract paintings and whimsical costumes create a party-like atmosphere. De la Prada uses her distinctive design sensibilities to provide excitement in every part of her collections. This has led her to be acknowledged as an authentic and original international voice.

Signature style:	*Playful, joyous designs; strong, clear visual theme statements*
Silhouettes:	*Comfortable*
Color palette:	*Bright, vivid colors. Each unit can emphasize a supplementary concept complementing the overall master collection concept.*

(opposite) Agatha Ruiz de la Prada, S/S 2018 collection.

Style, Voice, and Identity

An identity is a carefully crafted persona presented throughout your portfolio and your website, social media, leave-behind promotional materials, résumé, and business card. All of these materials are unified by one "voice"—consistent type usage, visual positioning, and image style. Together, these elements create your signature style.

Developing your own style requires time, experience, and confidence. As you plan, analyze your recent work to locate the strongest elements. Look at what stands out. Are you fascinated by textile texture? Do you work with color in a consistent or unexpected manner? How do you see silhouette and detail? What feature of your work do you want to highlight?

(below and opposite, top right) Ikshit Pande, QUOD F/W 2021–22.
(opposite, top and bottom left) Ikshit Pande, QUOD S/S 2020.
(opposite, bottom right) Ikshit Pande, QUOD F/W 2020–21.

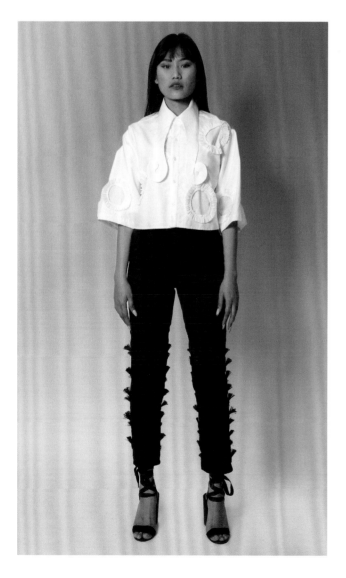

Review

The creative process is complex and non-linear. Inspiration can be stimulated but not called at will. As you work through conceptual ideas, rough sketches, mood boards, fabric boards, color stories, renderings, structure studies, and final sewn samples, your ideas will unfold and take shape.

Define your career desires as specifically as possible and analyze your audience from the outset of the creative process. Pay close attention to market segmentation and evolving conditions. Work to understand customer demographics: gender identification, age bracket, and lifestyle, culture, and spending habits. Ultimately your goal is to create a portfolio demonstrating that you understand how to merge skills, talent, personal direction, and market knowledge into a distinctive perspective.

Your portfolio will include a series of collections made up of individual units. Allow color and fabric stories, textures, and silhouettes to become organizing principles within units. Make sure every element of strategic personal positioning speaks with your unique voice. Use a consistent signature identity to demonstrate focused skills and talent.

Dos and Don'ts

Do be specific—understand and research your target market

Don't try to be all things to all people—take a creative position

Do be selective—retain only curated work that shows you at your best

Don't tell an inconsistent collection story

Do make your collection part of an overall portfolio strategy

Don't think of your design work as unrelated to your visual identity as a whole

Quick Quiz

- What are the standard parts of a customer profile?
- How can a sketchbook aid the concept development process?
- What are collection units?
- Why are mood and swatch boards important?
- What are the different uses of croquis, rendered sketches, and technical flats?

(opposite) Viktor & Rolf Haute Couture F/W 2015–16.

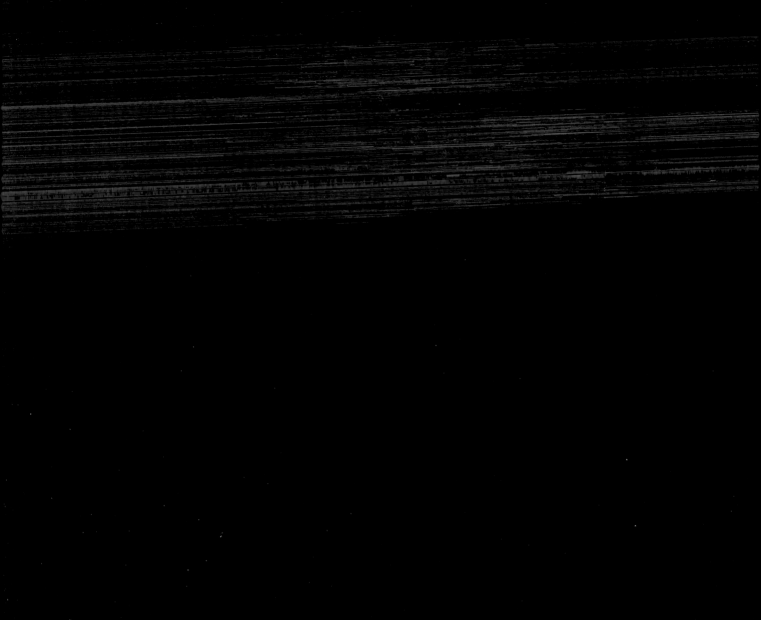

Concept to Content

Curating a fashion show and planning a portfolio share significant common elements, and both presentations are designed to showcase collections. Drama, a unified aesthetic, and an understanding of the target customer are essential in both.

Building a stand-out portfolio, just like all other opportunities to showcase design work, requires concentration, versatility, and vision. As boundaries have blurred across design fields, any aspiring designer must be willing to take on multiple roles to most effectively promote themself. To build a consistent narrative for your work and skills, you may assume the role of art director or graphic designer. Hiring the skills of a videographer or photographer may be required to fully express the individuality of your portfolio.

In this chapter, we look at the pathway from concept to final presentation. We begin with the role of rendering, digital skills, photography, and alternative media as they fit into portfolio planning. Finally, we examine the specifics of portfolio sequence and layout.

Building Portfolio Content

Rendering techniques

Rendering is the art of creating fully executed illustrations with color, shading, and texturing. There are many forms of rendering. The most common approaches in fashion are hand rendering and digital rendering, or a hybrid of the two. Conventional hand rendering may use pen or pencil drawings alone or with marker, paint, ink, watercolor, or gouache. In digital rendering, combinations of Adobe Photoshop and Illustrator are prevalent.

Any of these rendering techniques can be utilized in portfolio artwork as long as they indicate a significant level of mastery. Identify your strengths and weaknesses and choose accordingly. The field of fashion is extremely competitive; in a portfolio, demonstration of a unique perspective and excellent technique is important.

If you are skilled in several techniques, select illustrations based on your level of mastery and appropriateness. For example, watercolor may be more suitable for representing a transparent, soft texture such as chiffon, while for a thicker and opaque material, such as heavy-gauge knits or woven woolens, marker or gouache rendering may be a better choice. Seasonal designs could dictate selection of a particular technique. For maximum clarity and impact, focus on using the same rendering technique within each collection unit.

(below) Gianfranco Ferré line drawing ink sketch. "Inverso-white-shirt - circle".

Pen and pencil

Structural line drawings are the basis for all renderings. Pen or pencil can be used to fully execute final presentation renderings. Designers select pencil rendering for its delicacy, accuracy, and efficiency. It can be used in full color or only in black and white. Pencil combines well with watercolor and gouache to create emphasis or to highlight detail. It can be used to build lights and darks to create added dimension.

(below) Lamont O'Neal, fashion illustration in pencil.
(opposite) Sebastian Tjsie, line drawing.

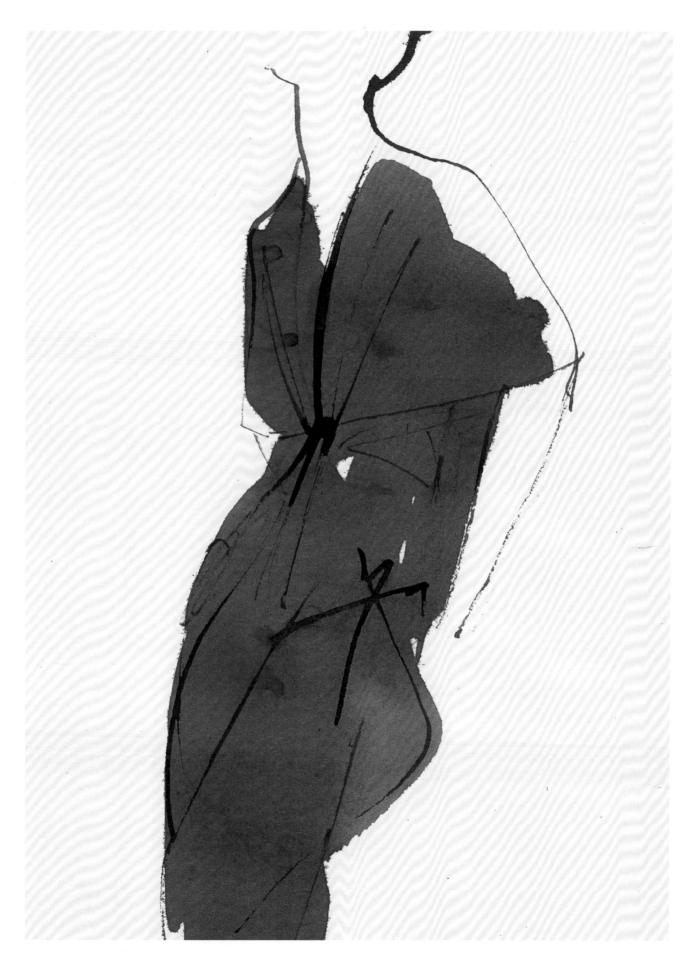

Watercolor and ink

As media, watercolor and ink behave similarly. The watercolor pigment that comes in either solid blocks or tubes can be diluted with water to provide various effects and color densities. Water-soluble ink is available in a bottled liquid form. Typical watercolor brushes are round, with long, absorbent natural or synthetic hairs. There is a wide array of shapes, sizes, and hair types to choose from, depending on personal preference. Whether a wet or dry brush technique is used, paper selection plays a significant role. The absorption qualities of different papers provide a variety of results. As proficiency develops, some artists favor a particular surface or texture of paper.

(opposite) Aurore de la Morinerie, watercolor illustration.
(right) Antonio Suarez, watercolor with color pencil accenting.

Rather than depicting technical details, fashion illustrators use watercolor and ink to illustrate the general silhouette as well as the feel and emotion of a garment (see also p.69 and 80). Because this technique requires additional time for mixing pigments and a significant drying period, it is often not a first choice for quick sketching.

(above) Dharti Patel, capsule collection, marker rendering and collage layout.

Markers

With ready-made and precise colors, marker rendering can become a portfolio cornerstone. This method is well suited to process sketches created during design development. Images can be produced quickly, present strongly, and represent a variety of materials well. Efficient, flexible, and immediate, the technique translates well to both screen and print.

Designers favor this method because it is the least time-consuming way to capture ideas in image form. While distinct colors are available, new colors can be created with application of color in layers. Marker is a clean media that dries almost instantly. When markers are the dominant media, colored pencils may be used in addition to provide finishing touches and create interesting accents and effects.

(above) Lishuang Xu, sketches for capsule collection When the SPACE Meets the BODY with marker rendering.

(right) Lishuang Xu, photos of capsule collection When the SPACE Meets the BODY.

(above) Stefan Radulescu, linoprint paper scraps collage technique.

(opposite) Cem Bora, fashion Illustration for *Vogue Italia*.

Collage and mixed media

The collage technique integrates a diverse range of materials into a single image. Materials can be culled from various sources: for example, internet images, magazine scans, or textile swatches. These may be used alongside markers or gouache. This technique offers another way of representing specific textural or textile design elements in fashion renderings, but is seldom used effectively to synthesize garment characteristics such as silhouettes and major construction lines.

Hybrid rendering

This form of rendering combines hand drawing with digitally generated images. A hybrid technique takes advantage of the best properties from each to create a stronger visual statement. In a commercial setting, the strengths of the artist, the desires of the client, and the situation dictate when to choose this type of mixed media. For portfolio, it is most meaningful as one of several techniques demonstrated.

(above) Tamara Albu, illustration 1, step 1. Hand drawing for poplin batiste cotton polka dot-print patterns.

(opposite, top left) Tamara Albu, illustration 1, step 2. Digital rendering and touch-ups in Adobe Photoshop.

(opposite, top right) Tamara Albu, illustration 1, step 3. Digital rendering and layout in Adobe Illustrator.

(opposite, bottom left) Tamara Albu, illustration 2, step 1. Hand drawing.

(opposite, bottom center) Tamara Albu, illustration 2, step 2. Digital rendering and touch-ups, Adobe Photoshop.

(opposite, bottom right) Tamara Albu, illustration 2, Step 3. Digital rendering and layout in Adobe Illustration.

POPLIN
BATISTE
COTTON
POLKA DOTS
PRINTED
PATTERN

LACE
VELVET
ORGANZA

Adobe Creative Suite

Adobe Creative Suite is a standard across all commercial design fields. Within this set of versatile programs, Photoshop and Illustrator are the two most widely used. For fashion designers, these programs work seamlessly together to digitally render and modify form. They easily allow for the matching of color, depiction of texture, addition of lighting effects, changes of scale, and adjustment to figure layout. In addition to individual garment rendering, specific producible textile and weave patterns can be developed or simulated.

InDesign is an Adobe Creative Suite module developed for page layout (including look-books, brochures, catalogs, or analog portfolios) and works well with the affiliated Photoshop and Illustrator programs often used for rendering.

Acrobat saves files from all Adobe Creative Suite programs into a PDF (portable document format). PDF works equally well for projected, emailable, or printed material.

Photoshop is a bitmap-based program which was initially developed to support and enrich photography techniques. Many industries have adapted its use to their own needs. The fashion industry routinely uses the program to create textile patterns, woven and knit textures, and to render or modify fashion sketches. The effects and tools in this program are particularly helpful in the simulation of complex patterns and textures in rendered sketches, as well as the digital assembly of portfolio pages.

Individual Adobe Creative Suite programs can be adapted to any designer's needs, from graphic or industrial design to fashion design. While not developed specifically for fashion CAD (computer-aided design), they are more affordable than specialized PLM (product lifecycle management) systems, allowing them to serve larger companies as well as medium and small-size design studios and independent freelancers.

(left) Jesse Evans, portfolio layout executed using Adobe InDesign.

(opposite) Jesse Evans, portfolio image rendered using Adobe Photoshop.

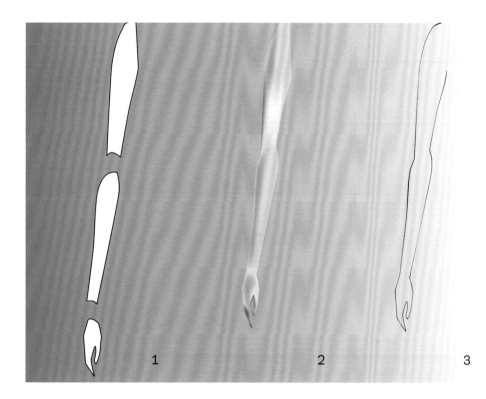

1 2 3

STEP 1
Draw the key body sections separated at the joints

STEP 2
Fill in the shapes with a skin tone; add light and shadow for 3D representation

STEP 3
Develop the accent outline, simulating drawing tool pressure

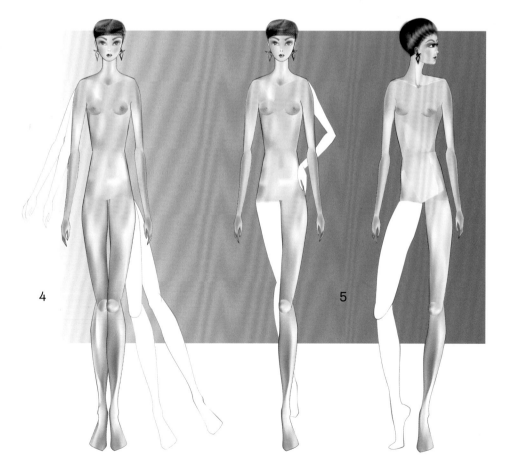

4 5

STEP 4
Assemble the completed sections into a straight pose

STEP 5
Choose poses of the arms and legs to flatter the garment

(opposite and above) Tamara Albu, garment and layout rendering in Adobe Illustrator.

Illustrator is a vector-based platform developed initially for graphic designers. It focuses on extreme precision in working with shapes, color effects, typography, and visual composition. As the software has evolved it has become essential to many industries, including the fashion field. Illustrator tools greatly simplify the creation of geometric patterns, rendering of stylized croquis, and production of technical drawings.

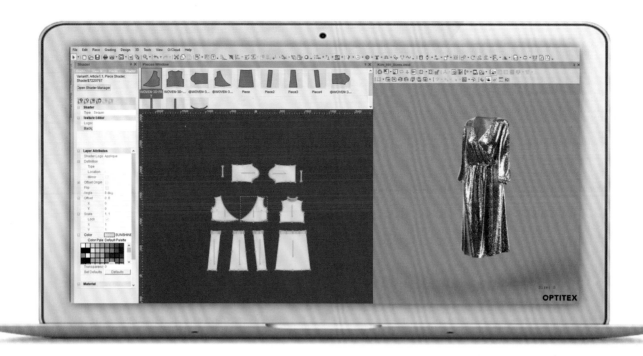

Specialized CAD (computer-aided design)

A variety of dedicated software enables designers to present their collections in a rendered format, even when analog drawing or painting is not a strength. Among the most prevalent software used in the industry are Kaledo by Lectra, EFI's Optitex, and YuniquePLM (part of Gerber's Design Suite). YuniquePLM allows the integration of some other digital platforms, such as Adobe Illustrator. Kaledo software is based on two fundamental concepts: creation and communication. Easy data transfer is built in between the four interconnected modules: Kaledo Collection, Kaledo Print, Kaledo Knit, and Kaledo Weave.

Unlike Adobe Photoshop and Illustrator, these complex PLM systems are specifically developed for the apparel manufacturing, fashion, and footwear industries. All of the software companies providing fashion design CAD offer a suite of modules supporting the entire development cycle. The system function includes: fabric and textile design; collection styles; technical sketches (flats); standard color palettes used for colorways; the cutting layout markers' configuration that calculates fabric waste reduction; the manufacturing technical package (tech pack) set of instructions, including the garment specification sheet (spec sheet) and grading (pattern alterations for each of the manufactured styles' sizes). Use depends heavily on company size and focused investment. For smaller companies with a limited budget, the more affordable alternative is non-dedicated software such as the Adobe Creative Suite.

(above, left, and opposite) Optitex: CAD—garment pattern, digital rendering. 3D-design simulation for Adobe Illustrator, showing multiple colorways and textile prints.

SPRING/SUMMER 2018

(opposite) Ikshit Pande, QUOD menswear collection S/S 2019.
(above) Elena Moussa, S/S 2018 line-up.

Look-books, line-sheets, and line-ups

The **look-book** is a digital or printed brochure containing all photographed garments created for a season. Each garment is photographed and styled on a model, using a minimal, neutral background (see also p. 127). Avoid anything that might distract the viewer. For easier identification, number/name each style and accompany this with a brief description of details, fabrication, and size. For the retail buyer, it is an informational catalog for assortment selection.

A **line-sheet** is a more functional document used in the ordering process. Fashion companies rely heavily on their look-books and line-sheets as reference material for buyers and as effective customer promotional material.

A **line-up** is a string of rendered sketches or photographs used as an overview of your style, emphasizing the relationships between the designs. Line-ups of sketches are often featured in portfolios as a way to show off a collection.

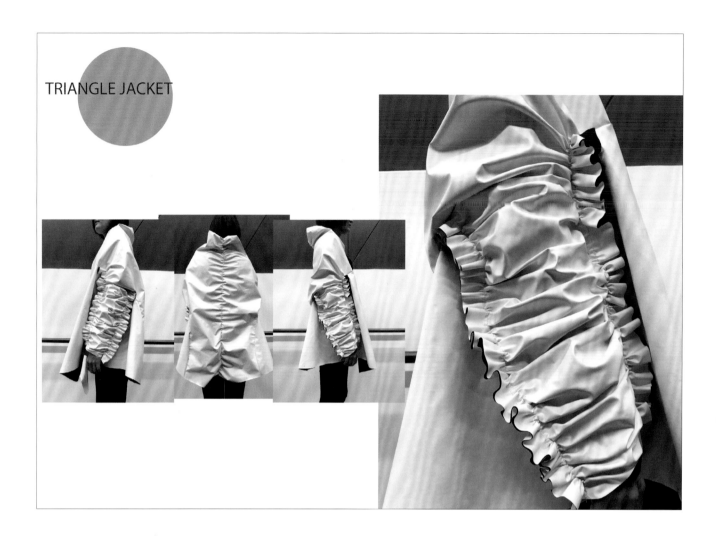

TRIANGLE JACKET

(above) Elena Moussa, Triangle Jacket.
(opposite) Ikshit Pande, QUOD F/W 2020–21.

Photographic imagery

Pairing two-dimensional sketches with development photographs of three-dimensional prototypes is an efficient way of documenting your designs during the making process. Muslin is commonly used for garment structural investigation. Depending on the construction, photography can be used to show a sequence of muslin (toile) variations pinned on the mannequin form, or to show garment fittings focusing on specific details best exemplified through final fabric. Some photographs document the development process. Others are meant to communicate the essence and emotional impact of the collection. There is no right or wrong way of telling a visual story. Final garments are often shot on models to clearly display notable attributes and their relationship to the body.

Curating Content

Effectively curating the portfolio in order to emphasize your strongest skills and perspective is key. This is achieved through focused selection. For every interview, increase your chances of establishing a strong connection with the interviewer by tailoring both the portfolio and any promotional material to the company's needs, strengths, and interests.

Make sure the portfolio demonstrates a clear understanding of fashion as a business. Be sure to integrate the factors below (discussed in Chapter 1):

· Comparable targeted customers
· Comparable price points
· Similar age group
· Matching market segment

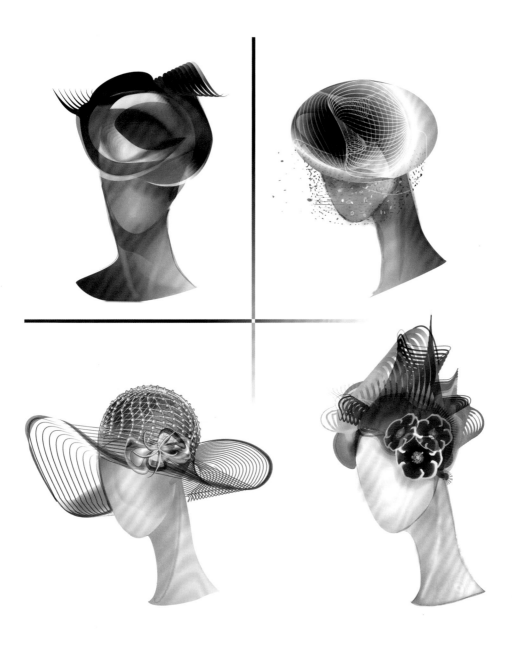

Collection organization by unit

A fashion collection is organized by units. Each unit becomes part of a cohesive collection statement within the portfolio: carefully plan layout, sketches, color and material swatches, and photographs to complement each other, as well as the overall portfolio concept.

Each unit will focus on specific designs. Surrounding elements such as background, title, and text must never overpower them. But, used properly, these surrounding elements will play an important role in enhancing the viewer's experience of the designs.

These elements must be carefully calibrated. For instance, using an excessively bold colored mood board as a backdrop for the designs or showing flats scaled too large diminishes the visual impact of your designs, taking away from your overall portfolio effect. When you balance elements properly the effect is memorable, stimulating, and engaging. Presentation of details, silhouettes, colors, and textures becomes the glue binding your collection and portfolio into a strong and cohesive statement.

Always include flats for at least some portfolio units. Flats are a must-have practical skill. Create a logical progression for introducing the material in each unit. You may choose to incorporate a title, a brief concept narrative, a mood board, rendered sketches, flats, and images documenting various stages of the development process.

Pose selection

Carefully consider the selection of a pose in both a croquis and a photograph. A pose should be chosen to flatter and show off specific garment design features. A dolman sleeve may require an extended arm, allowing the viewer to appreciate the sleeve's fullness. A pose showing motion may best demonstrate a contrasting color lining, or the float of a lightweight fabric. A group of designs using associated geometric and color combinations within the same silhouette may be best shown by utilizing the same straight pose. This combination of pattern and pose will help focus the viewer and emphasize innovative elements of your designs.

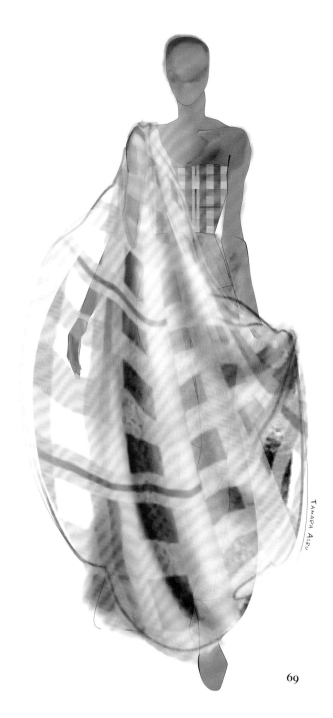

(opposite) Tamara Albu, millinery capsule collection.

(right) Tamara Albu, a pose selection demonstrating flowing fabric.

Editing content

Prepare to be flexible. Tailor the mix of elements to be included in each unit to support your overall portfolio goals. Edit, edit, edit! This is paramount in showing off your capabilities to their best advantage. Valuable content that doesn't fit in the portfolio may find a place on social media, as part of an email promotion, or as an interview follow-up.

Rendered sketches demonstrate both design and drawing skills. When tempted to eliminate rendered sketches, seriously consider the following:

· Will you have enough finished garments to present a solid collection?

· If your photography skills are not strong, will you need to hire a professional photographer?

· Will you be using professional models or presenting the garments on draping forms?

· Will you have access to the necessary accessories, a makeup artist, and a hair stylist? If not, will you be able to manage all of these on your own?

Block layout method

Our recommended block method of layout helps build a consistent visual story while allowing flexibility. You can use this method to mold a visual presentation that will best highlight your design skills, creativity, and originality.

A block is formed by one or multiple modules of a grid. A grid is an organized form of vertical and horizontal lines that helps partition a page into sections or blocks. These subdivisions create the basis of a modular and systematic methodology to the layout, especially for multipage records. They make the configuration process faster and ensure visual consistency between related pages. There are several types of grids:

· manuscript grids: predominantly used for blocks of text or images.

· column grids: used mostly in newspapers and magazines to organize multiple stories on the same page.

· hierarchical grids: where the modules are incrementally scaled up or down to signal a block ranking.

· modular grids: these are usually the ones recommended as a guide for portfolio layout.

The grid will be discussed further in Chapter 3.

(opposite, top) Block layout, portrait orientation.

(opposite, below) Block layout, portrait orientation; Djiun Wang content.

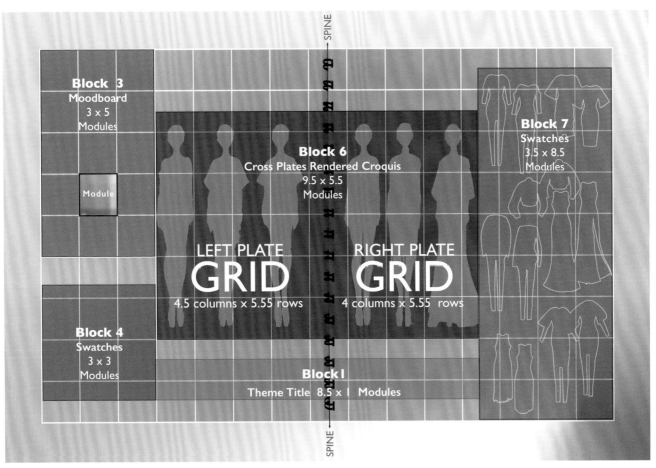

Block 3
Moodboard
3 x 5
Modules

Module

Block 6
Cross Plates Rendered Croquis
9.5 x 5.5
Modules

LEFT PLATE
GRID
4.5 columns x 5.55 rows

RIGHT PLATE
GRID
4 columns x 5.55 rows

Block 7
Swatches
3.5 x 8.5
Modules

Block 4
Swatches
3 x 3
Modules

Block I
Theme Title 8.5 x I Modules

SPINE

SPINE

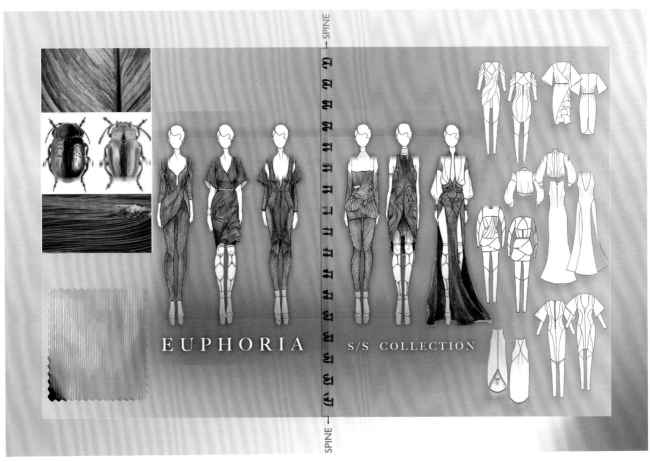

E U P H O R I A   S/S COLLECTION

SPINE

SPINE

SPINE

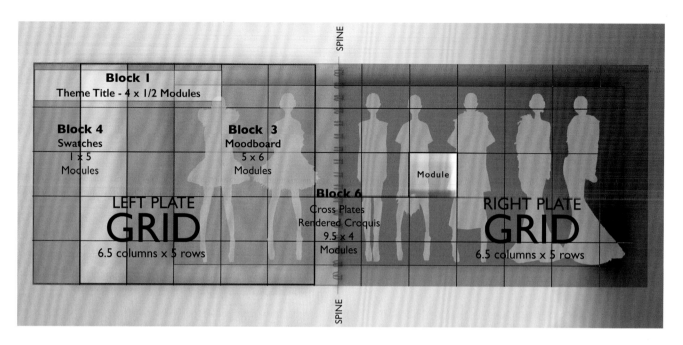

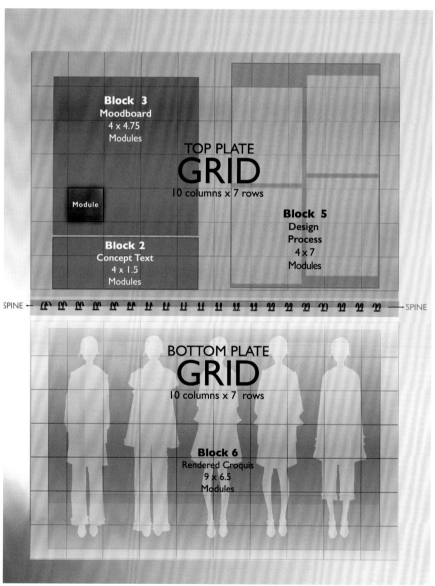

(above) Block layout, horizontal landscape orientation.

(right) Block layout, vertical landscape orientation.

Spontaneity was one of main characteristics in Jean Dubuffet's work.
I applied his approach of spontaneity and combined it
with one of his technique for creating his artworks, whitch is collage.
I created this draping collage and exploring and experimenting with it
without thinking.
The result shows various silhouette and details that i had never thought
of prior to the experimentation.

(above) Block layout, horizontal landscape orientation; Djiun Wang content.

(left) Block layout, vertical landscape orientation; Sebastian Tjsie content.

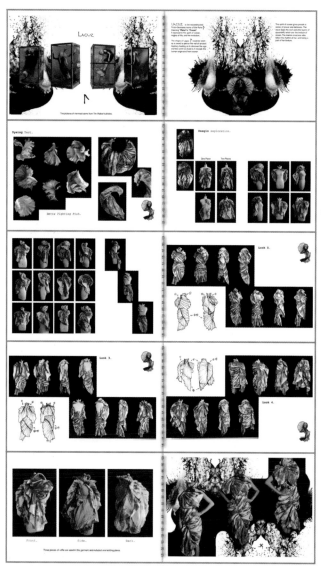

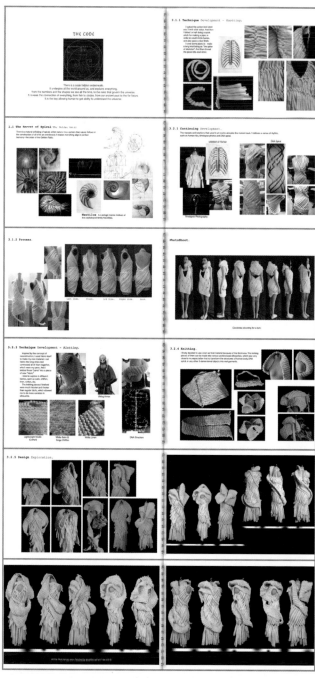

(top left) Jingwen Xie, portfolio intro page.

(top right) Jingwen Xie, portfolio first unit, selected plates.

(above) Jingwen Xie, portfolio last unit, selected plates.

(right) Jingwen Xie, portfolio closing page.

Portfolio Configuration

When asked about expectations for recent graduates applying for positions, Oscar de la Renta indicated he was not interested in looking at "school portfolios". He meant a body of artwork or projects created during a student's years of study. Portfolios prepared with a consistent concept, "a story," were preferred. He was looking for portfolios that showed a clear understanding of the fashion concept, inspiration, color and fabric sense, creativity, and originality: the same elements he valued in a fashion collection. A well presented portfolio allows a viewer to easily "read" a designer's skills and perspective.

A well-designed, thoughtful portfolio guides the viewer through your vision as a designer. A portfolio is a story with sequence. It is a summary of your creativity and skills that can be read as a book. Whatever form it takes, whether it is analog or digital, focus on curation and functional sequence is required. Your signature style guides the story to become a dramatic curated narrative with a unified aesthetic. It is plotted, visualized, and laid out around a style and an overall presentation idea. A unit is a chapter moving the plot forward; each will be based on a different inspiration or theme. Individually, each unit needs to be strong enough to stand alone yet consistent enough to support the overall portfolio concept. A grand finale makes a strong closing to your portfolio, just as it does at a live fashion show.

The framework below provides a solid portfolio structure. The portfolio is divided into four broad sections: introduction, core portfolio concept, themed groups (or units), and theme finale.

1. Introduction: the first theme group uses a strong color theme to grab attention and mark the beginning of the portfolio—the dramatic entrance.

2. Core concept: the concept behind the portfolio drives the plot.

3. Chapters: portfolio units.

4. Conclusion: grand finale—the memorable exit.

Portfolio section structure

Based on your chosen concept and the research done prior to fabric selection, you will decide on several color stories. Each color story is supported by a distinct inspiration or theme. The initial flow of color stories will help you clearly organize your collection. There are two major methods for ordering the themes: alternation and progression. Just as a well-balanced collection is supported by strong strategic planning from the earliest development stages, so the process of designing a successful portfolio requires precision planning.

A range of preferred fabrication techniques, color palettes, design details, and overall personal aesthetics are the building blocks of a successful collection (see Chapter 1, p.27) and portfolio. How you group and sequence those elements will determine how the viewer will move through your portfolio. One of the portfolio's purposes is to grab the viewer's attention and hold it with each new page. To achieve this, the element of surprise is essential. Strategically, you must place the two most captivating units of the entire portfolio as the first and last units of your story sequence. The first one will create a striking entrance, announcing your signature style, while the last one will conclude the story through a "grand finale" meant to be remembered long after the interview is over. The middle units add convincing evidence of your knowledge and technical skills, as well as showing your creativity, talent, and ingenuity; they reinforce an understanding of your versatility. The plot (portfolio concept) explains the story of the designer's overall vision and concept. As the plot proceeds, more is revealed, creating a deeper understanding of the story. All elements together create a unified, strong, and clear narrative.

By alternating or progressing the color stories from unit to unit, excitement will be maintained. When deciding how to structure your portfolio, a preliminary consideration is whether to opt for alternation or progression. Whichever technique you choose, be careful not to ever compromise your unique vision while demonstrating a full range of your abilities. There is a fine balance between maintaining your authenticity and showcasing your versatility.

Alternation method

Alternation places themes with their relevant color stories, patterns, and fabrication in an alternating pattern. Following the manner in which fashion shows are curated, the mood changes with each new group of garments. For example:

- THEME 1: an inspiring unit of silks in black and white
- THEME 2: a gracious, quieter section of light, sweet pastels
- THEME 3: profusive darker floral prints in lightweight cottons
- THEME 4: a softer and sophisticated unit of brushed jerseys in muted tones of dusted beige, blues, and purples
- THEME 5: Jacquards in deep jewel tones of sapphire and emerald
- GRAND FINALE: the collection concludes with a vibrant color story. Imagine a climax of iridescent metallic fabrics, moiré gold and copper taffetas with deep violet chiffons

PORTFOLIO SECTION STRUCTURE
Alternation method

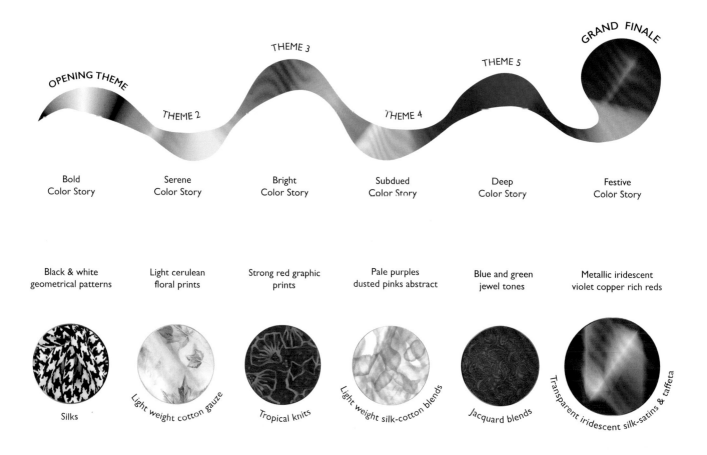

| Bold Color Story | Serene Color Story | Bright Color Story | Subdued Color Story | Deep Color Story | Festive Color Story |

| Black & white geometrical patterns | Light cerulean floral prints | Strong red graphic prints | Pale purples dusted pinks abstract | Blue and green jewel tones | Metallic iridescent violet copper rich reds |

Silks — Light weight cotton gauze — Tropical knits — Light weight silk-cotton blends — Jacquard blends — Transparent iridescent silk-satins & taffeta

Progression method

Progression follows a narrative structure. The portfolio concept is plotted in the same manner as a novel or a movie script. A summer resort collection story may follow the chronology of specific events of the day. For example:

- THEME 1: a clean, crisp morning with a palette of light, sky-blue piqué, still with subtle impact
- THEME 2: a quiet afternoon in calm, neutral tones of warm grays and beiges
- THEME 3: an intense summer sunset of deeper reds and purples: soft, smooth, lightweight cashmere
- THEME 4: a dark, breezy night by the sea in deep blues and aquamarines of textured brocades, accented by thin veins of white, reminiscent of ruffled sea-foam
- THEME 5: escalates to the grand finale, perhaps describing a lavish, glamorous party in the exquisite copper and gold metallic and jewel tones of iridescent taffeta and silks

PORTFOLIO SECTION STRUCTURE
Progression method

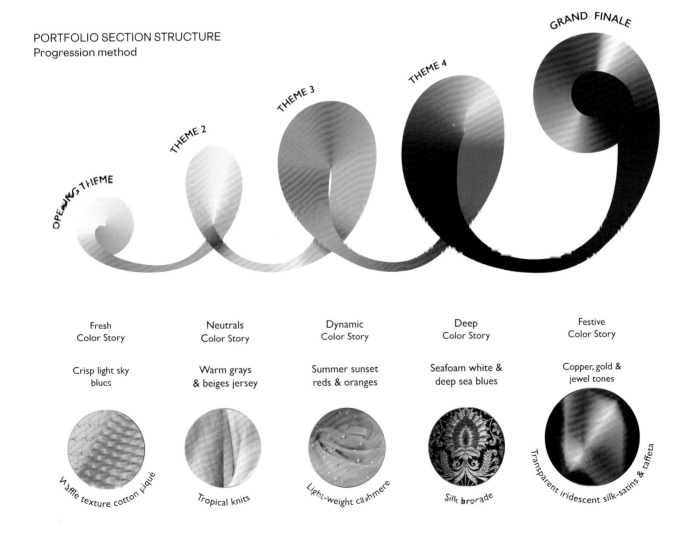

Fresh Color Story	Neutrals Color Story	Dynamic Color Story	Deep Color Story	Festive Color Story
Crisp light sky blues	Warm grays & beiges jersey	Summer sunset reds & oranges	Seafoam white & deep sea blues	Copper, gold & jewel tones

Waffle texture cotton piqué · Tropical knits · Light-weight cashmere · Silk brocade · Transparent iridescent silk-satins & taffeta

Supplementary Material

If particular work definitely does not integrate into your basic portfolio concept, put it aside, retaining it for future use. Consider selecting this alternative work to become part of your personal promotional material (see p.121-3 and p. 134). For example, it could be featured in a targeted leave-behind brochure or series of postcards prepared specifically for an interview. It might become part of a sequence of email PDFs supporting your search for a position with a specific employer. Use this material to speak directly to an employer's interest without diluting the clarity of your core portfolio.

Leave-behind or follow-up materials continue to communicate your value to an interviewer after you have concluded an interview. Utilize typography and visual layout elements matching your portfolio in these promotional materials. Whether you choose to create a series of postcards, an emailable PDF, or a brochure, reinforce your visual and conceptual story.

As you make whatever visual adjustments are necessary to fit material into your chosen promotional format, it is paramount to maintain consistency. Within this supplementary material, the project sequence is not as critical as it is in your portfolio. You are creating an enticing sampling of your skills for prospective employers. A capsule collection based on a period in fashion history may be followed by a contemporary textile design developed in CAD. This could precede a collection of technical sketches and specs. For the benefit of the employer, projects should be easily identified with tags and titles.

(opposite) Joan Dominique, garment and accessories promotional material.

Review

Navigate carefully between analog and digital techniques. In the case of original hand-rendered artwork, the designer concept is continued in a tactile presence through the choice of paper and other surfaces. Fully digital and hybrid artwork presents the opportunity to demonstrate alternative skills (see p.56).

A well-designed, thoughtful portfolio guides the viewer through your vision as a designer. Your portfolio should be divided into a narrative of four broad sections: introduction, core concept, theme groups, and theme finale.

Use a selection of fabrication techniques, color palettes, design details, and garment groupings to describe your personal aesthetic while showcasing commercial skills.

When creating a portfolio, hold the viewer's interest with the unpredictable and unexpected, anchored by the consistent. In setting up a presentation sequence, work with either alternation or progression. In all communication, be clear and consistent.

Dos and Don'ts

Do put your portfolio in an organized, logical four-part sequence

Don't be inconsistent in communicating your skills and perspective

Do ruthlessly review and reevaluate successful past projects

Don't let attachment to particular projects prevent focused editing

Do reinforce your personal aesthetic and story in every part of the portfolio

Don't downplay your own uniqueness by telling a predictable story

Quick Quiz

1. Why should a particular rendering technique be chosen?

2. On what basis should content be curated?

3. What are the four sections of a standard portfolio configuration?

4. What is the block layout method?

5. What are the two methods for visually presenting a collection discussed in this chapter?

(opposite) Aurore de la Morinerie, John Galliano for Maison Margiela Couture 2015.

Portfolio Styles

Your portfolio should aim to impress not just with completed work but also with the skills used to achieve that work. While it provides insight into inspiration, it also shows process. This should be kept in mind when deciding upon rendering techniques and upon analog or digital portfolio formats.

Reaching the right audience also requires the right tool. The marketplace is an important consideration when evaluating options within analog and digital formats. While personal websites allow review at the convenience of the viewer, an analog portfolio works especially well in intimate one-to-one settings. In this situation it is easiest to fully appreciate the skill and detail of hand rendering, and the tactile quality of fabric swatches. The analog portfolio becomes a holistic material experience.

A convincing portfolio must be based on your strengths as well as presentation needs. Objective assessment of both visual and technical skills is part of the job of overall curation. Often designers choose to create complementary analog and digital portfolios, each demonstrating designer strengths while maximizing format strengths.

Analog Portfolio

An analog portfolio is a physical book or box that includes original artwork or high-quality printouts of scanned art. It provides physical evidence of a designer's competency. In an industry where touch and personal choice are decisive factors, it is an intimate tactile object demonstrating an individual's point of view.

When planning an analog portfolio, the designer has complete control from cover to cover, selecting size, paper, and style to reflect their own aesthetics. You are not limited by templates as you might be in a digital setting. This type of portfolio is an immediate, immersive experience without the distractions of sidebar advertisements. Software, device, and internet problems do not interfere with accessing and appreciating the work.

Leverage the physical as much as possible in developing an analog portfolio. This is a package where content meets material to demonstrate a design perspective. The selection of a portfolio case style instantly reflects your visual preferences as a designer. For instance, those presenting a modern look may seek a sleek binder surface as a reflection of its contemporary, polished content.

Certain distinctive hand skills (see pp. 48-55) are best demonstrated in an analog portfolio. For instance, the paper surface and texture of a watercolor illustration may not be fully experienced in a digital reproduction. The skill of this method is most clearly shown through original material. In this case, design creativity and technical excellence come together to create a competitive edge.

(below) Three-piece hidden screwpost binding portfolio and slipcase, Mullenberg Designs.

Selecting a portfolio case

You will select a portfolio case based on your aims as well as budget. We recommend selecting a case that is small and light enough to carry easily. Choose a material that is durable and elegant—artificial leather and bookbinding linen wear well.

A series of easily available, premade book-style binders in varying sizes are available, or you may choose to have a binder or box made to your own specifications by contacting a specialty vendor (see pp. 88-9). Always consider functionality. Custom cases made of acrylic can easily be damaged, and aluminum cases may fingerprint or scratch more than you would like.

Choose a binder that allows for easy editing and updating by selecting a portfolio case with removable sleeve pages. Consider the experience of the viewer as well as portfolio maintenance. Does your artwork remain clean and well protected? Are the pages easy to turn? Are the images easily and fully visible? Ease of viewing and interaction are extremely important during interviews.

The most common portfolio cases contain about 20 pages, referred to as plates. The left and right plates together form a spread. The binding system that holds the plates together is called the spine.

(below) Easily available standard portfolio cases with handles.

Available choices for portfolio cases include:

Stock

- Ring-bound binders—various sizes and styles of artificial leather
- Screwpost binders—various sizes and styles of artificial leather

Custom

- Three-piece hidden screwpost binder— fabric bound
- Slipcase—fabric bound with multi-page portfolio
- Connected clamshell presentation box— fabric bound
- Unconnected clamshell presentation box— fabric bound
- Half clamshell or magnetic flap case— fabric bound
- Hinged binder—aluminum
- Frosted or opaque screwpost binder—acrylic

The pages in ring binders are easiest to manipulate and turn. If selecting a screwpost binder, be aware that this form of binding limits the ability of a book to lie flat, which will affect your layout choices. On the plus side, multiple screw lengths offer increased editing flexibility. As you edit your portfolio, changing the length of the screw may accommodate a modified number of plates. Box-style portfolios allow pages to be lifted out and examined individually.

Many choices of standard premade portfolios are available for purchase online. Prat Paris offers a wide selection of hardbound press books and spiral binders in an assortment of sizes. Itoya binders are common in the United States and Japan. Other hard- and soft-bound binders are available online or from stationery vendors. The supplied pages in Prat Paris binders are usually frosted and scratch resistant. If you have the option of clear or frosted sleeves, frosted sleeves are preferable for durability. Brands such as Pina Zangaro or Mullenberg Designs offer an assortment of more expensive customizable structures. These may be custom-stamped or detailed for an additional cost.

By setting your work apart from the standardization of the screen, a well-conceived and executed analog portfolio emphasizes craft and individuality. It allows for greater integration of physical elements that can more fully speak of the importance and material aspects of both ornament and fabric.

When considering a physical portfolio, think of the values you want to project. The special texture of a paper or handmade binding techniques may be appropriate if craftsmanship and artisan work are of primary importance in either the work shown or the companies to be approached. Remember, in either case, that together the quality of the work shown and manner of presentation promote the designer. Always keep in mind that your work must never be upstaged by its presentation format.

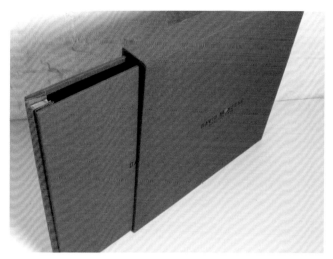

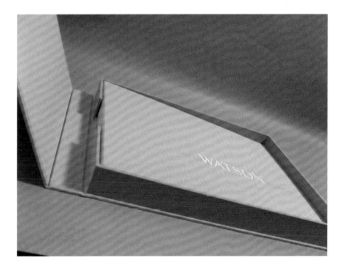

(top left) Print portfolio/iPad case: three-piece hidden screwpost binding portfolio and slipcase, fabric bound.

(top right) David McNeese portfolio: three-piece portfolio and slipcase. Italiano slate with Italiano black lining on the book and orange lining inside the slate-gray slipcase.

(center left) Ransom full-case portfolio and slipcase.

(center right) Two-piece clamshell portfolio and slipcase, fabric bound.

(left) Half clamshell with magnetic flap, debossed: white and gray on the book, blind debossed on slipcase.

Courtesy Mullenberg Designs.

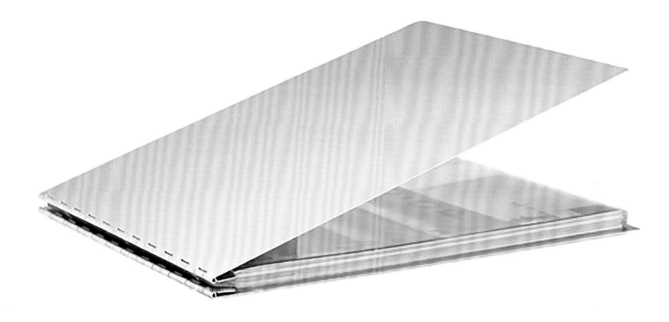

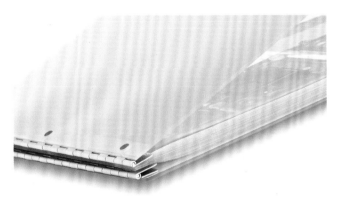

(top) Custom-format Machina anodized aluminum screwpost binder.

(center left) Frosted acrylic portfolio cover with aluminum screwpost binder.

(center right) Custom aluminum portfolio case, anodized laser etched.

(left) Acrylic screwpost portfolio book, onyx (matte black).

Courtesy Pina Zangaro.

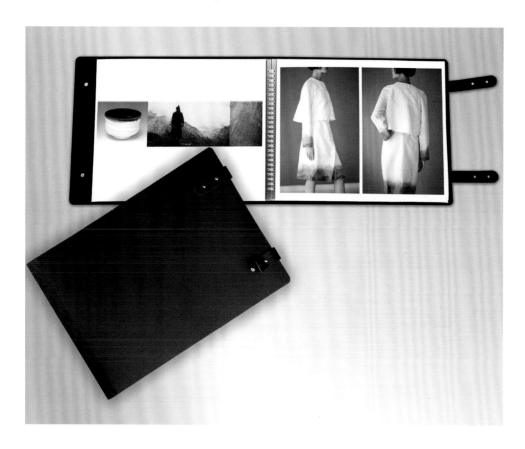

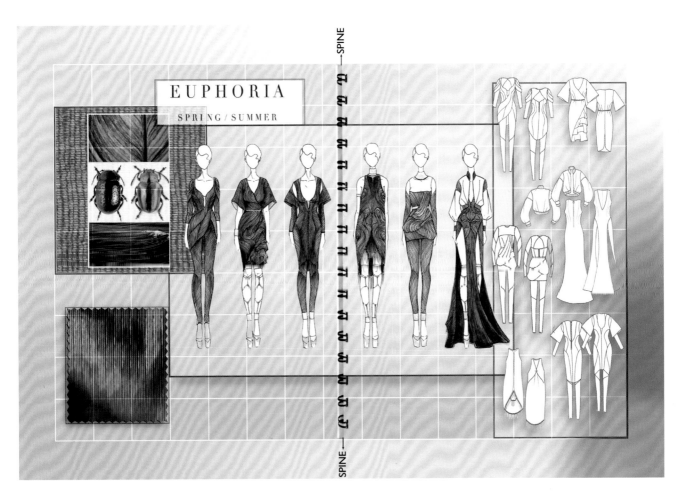

(opposite, above) Zipper portfolio case with handles, portrait orientation, featuring Minori Amada.

(opposite, below) Portfolio with strap closure, landscape orientation, featuring Louise Hidinger.

(top) Example of portfolio spread in portrait orientation, featuring Djiun Wang.

(above) Example of portfolio spread in landscape orientation, featuring Dyanna Csaposs.

Digital Portfolio

A portfolio may be shared on an umbrella portfolio site such as the social media platform Behance, or be created as a stand-alone personal site with a hosting site such as Squarespace. All digital sites have the advantage of immediate accessibility for the viewer, as well as the ability to incorporate contact linking, motion, and sound.

Portfolio hosting website

A well-designed umbrella site such as Behance.net and Coroflot.com increases visitor traffic, providing broader exposure. Behance is an Adobe platform built specifically for showcasing the portfolios of creative professionals. With its comprehensive approach, the site has developed an active social network. It not only offers visibility to skilled visual professionals, but also includes a tab of job postings.

Companies looking to recruit can browse a selection of skilled designers to fit their aesthetics, price point, and customer profile. Emailing weblinks allows a designer to focus a viewer on any particularly relevant work.

Originality, creativity, and presentation play a crucial role in making your portfolio stand out in this market environment. Get acquainted with the "competition". To be most effective, focus must remain on a defined client (unique targeted market, customer profile, type of company, and price point). A signature style and consistent presentation of designer identity lead to a clearly focused portfolio able to attract attention and potentially generate interview opportunities. Before making a site selection, carefully evaluate other work showcased. Are you in good company? To remain relevant and competitive, make sure your site content is regularly updated.

(left and below) Behance and Coroflot are digital portfolio hosting sites that may be accessed on assorted digital devices.

(right) Katrin Schnabl website, Orient collection.

(right, below) Katrin Schnabl website, costume design for Joffrey Ballet, "Beyond the Shore".

Your own portfolio website

A clear visual understanding of a designer's aesthetics and easy, functional navigation are defining assets in a personal web portfolio. You will need to decide on a presentation strategy to make your site an enticing visitor experience. It may contain a gallery of artwork, or a number of collections divided by season and year. Web-builder services such as Portfolio. adobe.com, Wix.com, Fabrik.io, Foliolink.com, and Squarespace.com provide tools (including website templates) to aid users in creating highly personalized websites. In selecting, always consider long- and short-term cost, the ease and versatility of tools, and site reliability (proper maintenance and technical support). You can pull up your website for reference during a job interview or provide the link after discussing a project with a potential client.

Website Content Impact

Whether you are choosing a hosting site or building a personal webpage, keep the following factors in mind:

- Keep it neat, well-organized, and easy to navigate.

- Curate your artwork. Less is more. The website is not a complete inventory of your creative output. The website gives the visitor an idea of your personal style, design affinities, and aesthetic directions. These visuals function as teasers; specifics can be revealed during the job interview or client briefing.

- The graphic presentation should match your style as a designer, yet never overshadow the collection content.

Adapting web pages for mobile devices

Most web builders now provide the ability to adapt the page layout for mobile devices, such as phones and tablets. Since mobile is now a common way of accessing the world, make sure to test that your content visualizes well for mobile apps. Depending on the web builder chosen, you may need to pay attention to specifically adapting content for mobile readiness. While a small phone screen is not the optimum device to show off work during a job interview, it might be a useful way to take advantage of unpredictable circumstances. Spontaneous informal site browsing by potential employers or contacts can lead to unexpected opportunities.

(above) Tamara Albu, digital portfolio presentation of the same content for multiple digital devices.

(opposite) Elena Moussa's portfolio viewed on laptop and mobile phone. Correctly designed portfolio webpages become adaptable for multiple mobile devices.

(below) Céline Haddad's website homepage viewed on a desktop monitor.

Portfolio Layout and Composition

Good organization of visual space helps a viewer in absorbing a portfolio. Guidelines for visual presentation should be considered early in the process, be it for analog or digital portfolio. While a polished, professional portfolio is always the end product of focused vision and curated selection, different layout applications, composition, and graphic elements apply specifically to each type of portfolio.

Text, mood board, swatch panel, background, or technical sketches must be carefully calibrated. Although each surrounding element may play its role in enhancing the viewer experience, they must never dominate the designs. Colors that are too intense in a mood board or flats that are too large may compete with the designs instead of complementing them.

Format and resolution

An alternate means of digital viewing can be a multi-page PDF or PowerPoint. Image selection can be derived from either an analog or digital portfolio. These documents have the advantage of being able to include hyperlinks, sound, animation, and video clips.

Once an analog portfolio is finalized, the images can be optimized for digital use. The illustrations are scanned, cleaned, and resaved in various formats and resolutions. It is very important to establish the purpose of digitized files. If final images are intended to be commercially printed, the minimum resolution should not be below 300 dpi at the size they will be printed. Anything lower than that may cause pixelation in reproduction. EPS, TIFF, and PDF work well as file formats for any form of printable materials.

Files intended for projected presentations are fine at a resolution of 200 dpi. Images meant exclusively for website content usually have a resolution of 72 dpi. Websites will work best with images such as GIFs, JPEGs, or PNGs. If a website image resolution is too high, that image might take too long to load. When someone is browsing your site, excessive waiting time could cause loss of interest.

Grid

A very useful way to create a well-balanced page in both analog and digital portfolios is to develop a grid template or, in the case of a digital portfolio, to select one of the templates provided by the hosting site. Adobe Portfolio refers to their grid templates as "themes". A good resource for grid template examples is portfolio.adobe.com/themes. Grids are meant as guides to ensure that website browsing and navigation are both functional and pleasant. They keep the columns, margins, website buttons, and text alignments consistent throughout your web pages.

Grids are about both making and breaking rules. They underpin a layout, providing strong, unnoticed guidance. You may be guided by symmetric or asymmetric grids. Symmetric grids follow a center line, utilizing equal columns, rows, and margins to guide element placement. Within an asymmetric grid, margins and columns can be different from one another.

Choosing a modular-style grid (symmetrical or asymmetrical) allows for easy manipulation of elements in an organized manner. The results are a series of easy-to-read, consistent pages. Your layout choices should never become dry or rigid. The satisfaction of the viewer experience benefits from unexpected visual twists and the element of surprise. Consistent should never be allowed to become dull. Take the viewer by surprise. Break the mold occasionally to create additional impact.

(opposite) Modular grids—landscape orientation.

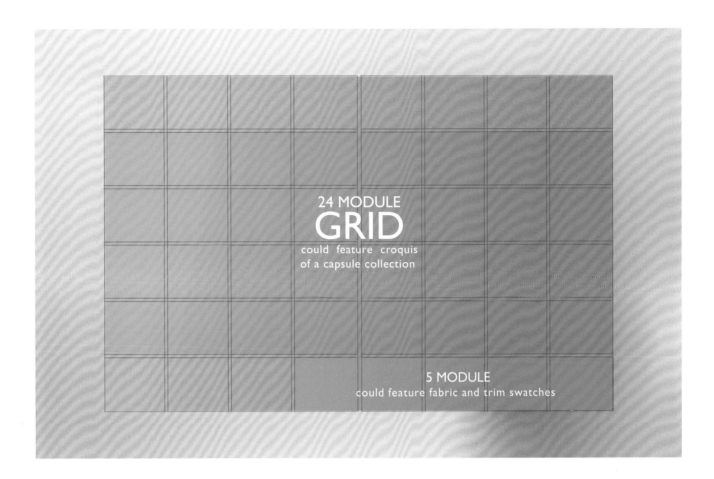

24 MODULE
GRID
could feature croquis
of a capsule collection

5 MODULE
could feature fabric and trim swatches

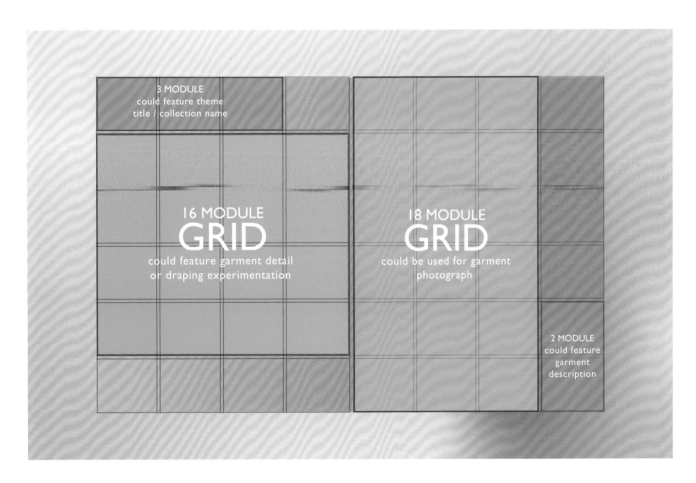

3 MODULE
could feature theme
title / collection name

16 MODULE
GRID
could feature garment detail
or draping experimentation

18 MODULE
GRID
could be used for garment
photograph

2 MODULE
could feature
garment
description

Orientation

For an analog portfolio, you are free to choose either portrait or landscape orientation. Once chosen, orientation should be kept consistent throughout your portfolio. Most designers prefer landscape orientation since it allows designs to be presented alongside one another, mimicking the fashion show finale where the whole collection may be viewed at a glance.

In online environments, variation in viewing formats will heavily impact what material you select. Be aware that most cell phone content will be viewed vertically, while computer-viewed material will most often be seen horizontally. Tablet material may be viewed in either orientation.

Background

Your creativity and skills are always most important. Whether you decide to select a solid color, choose an image related to the collection, utilize a theme borrowed from your mood board, or work with an abstract pattern as your background, nothing should ever visually overpower the designs you are presenting. For each unit theme, the focal point must be its designs.

In both analog and digital formats, consistent layout helps a viewer navigate multiple collections and immediately understand the guiding perspective of the designer. Background choices help create visual unity throughout a portfolio. Awareness of balance is essential. After choosing a background direction, feel free to manipulate it to best showcase your work. Deciding on page backgrounds could demand background tone variation or the ghosting of a photographic image. To highlight a group of designs on the same spread, you may choose to modify portions or the entire background with transparency, masking, or other effects in Photoshop. Both Photoshop and Illustrator can be of great assistance in controlling and maintaining a unified, impactful visual presentation.

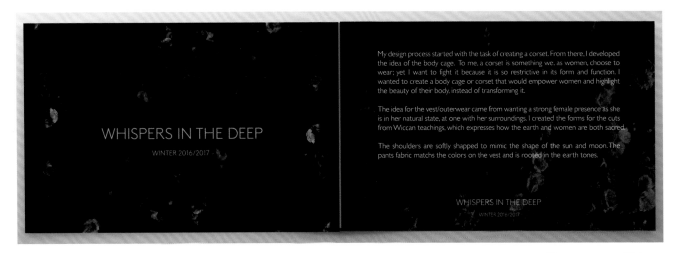

WHISPERS IN THE DEEP

WINTER 2016/2017

My design process started with the task of creating a corset. From there, I developed the idea of the body cage. To me, a corset is something we, as women, choose to wear; yet I want to fight it because it is so restrictive in its form and function. I wanted to create a body cage or corset that would empower women and highlight the beauty of their body, instead of transforming it.

The idea for the vest/outerwear came from wanting a strong female presence as she is in her natural state, at one with her surroundings. I created the forms for the cuts from Wiccan teachings, which expresses how the earth and women are both sacred.

The shoulders are softly shapped to mimic the shape of the sun and moon. The pants fabric matchs the colors on the vest and is rooted in the earth tones.

WHISPERS IN THE DEEP

WINTER 2016/2017

(above) Dyanna Csaposs, portfolio spreads with mood board as a backdrop to featured designs.

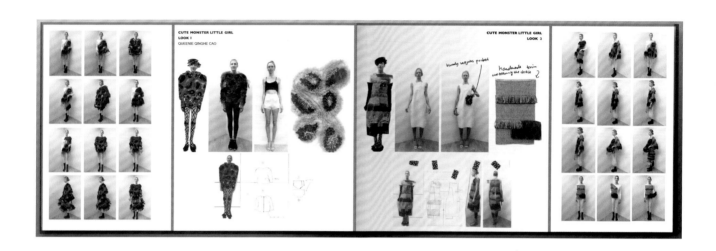

(above) Queenie Qinghe Cao, portfolio spread utilizing grid-module geometry for layout composition.

(opposite, top) Pauline Hilborn, portfolio utilizing dimmed background image, placing the focus on the garment designs.

(opposite, below) Tamara Albu, portfolio utilizing contrasting color block background to highlight rendered sketches.

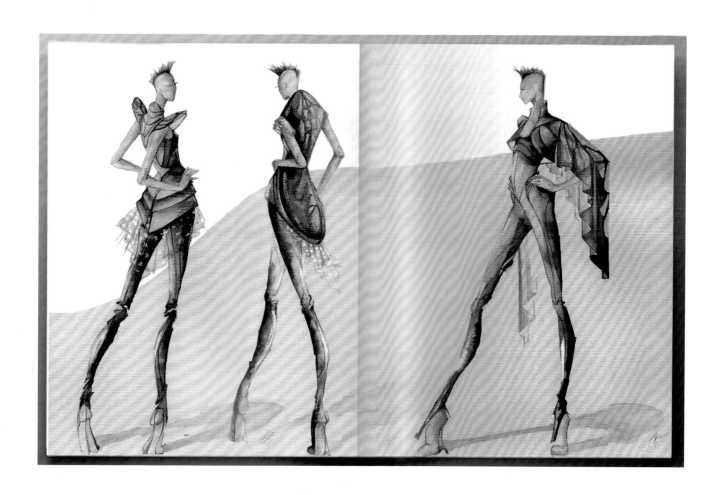

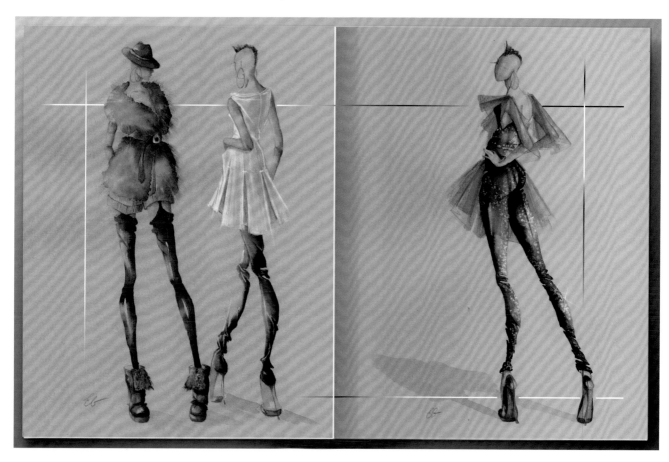

Review

The portfolio demonstrates process, final product, and a personal perspective. Just as a web portfolio speaks the designer's visual language, so the physical quality of a designer's analog portfolio must complement its contents in style, attitude, and polish.

Both digital and analog portfolios are interactive experiences. The analog portfolio makes the most of physical attributes. Original hand-rendered artwork with distinctive qualities or techniques works particularly well in this format. An online digital portfolio, on the other hand, has the advantage of being able to include hyperlink insertions and animated or kinetic media.

Recent years have seen a huge increase in the amount of work conducted remotely. Portable, quickly updatable web portfolios fit this context well. To make the most of all available opportunities, designers should consider using both analog and digital formats in conjunction.

Whichever format it is in, your portfolio should always aim to show excellence and vision.

Dos and Don'ts

Do choose analog or digital, or a combination of both, for your portfolio based on the strengths of your media

Don't allow technical needs to outweigh curation for quality

Do realize that your portfolio style is part of an overall strategy

Don't try to show all your work on a webpage or website

Do be selective in curating content and choosing a website host

Don't forget to make sure your website has mobile capability

Quick Quiz

- Why is it important to pay attention to file resolution for both analog and digital portfolios?

- What advantage does a digital portfolio offer over an analog portfolio?

- What are the two most important aspects to consider when designing your personal digital website?

- What are the benefits of structuring your layout using a grid?

(opposite, top) Eleonora Gendler, Chrysalis costume, background cutout.

(opposite, below) Eleonora Gendler, partial border background on grid.

CHAPTER 4

Personal Branding

Strategy
Define Your Look
Applying Branding to Media

Your personal brand is a combination of experience, skills, and attitude. It is your story told consistently in your voice. Decide what your core messages are and stick to them. Be true to those values. Your brand image establishes expectations and makes promises to employers and customers.

Visually, personal brand is manifested as an outward image, positioning you for success. This image statement includes impactful use of logo, type, and color. All graphic design choices, photographic styling, and personal presentation become part of your story. Résumé, business card, stationery, social media, and website must speak with one unified voice.

As a designer evolves, personal branding evolves. The process begins as you plan for entry into the fashion industry, but brand and marketing strategy, coupled with image, will become a lifelong series of refinements. The strength of your personal brand becomes an essential part of cultivating your career.

Strategy

(above) Betty Kim (Joo Eun Kim), self promotion material.

Strong strategy integrates values, concept, pictorial image, and assorted media (digital and printed) to reinforce your credibility, propelling you forward. Branding is about strategy. Well-planned marketing and branding serves to enhance your professional profile and set you apart. Create material that showcases your skills using finely targeted visual language. You are looking to create a solid connection with potential employers that is both emotional and skills-based.

Focus

You have already worked on developing a consistent customer profile (see p.13-5). Use that knowledge to tie together your overall skill set, values, and style into a coordinated career approach. A clearly defined audience will help you create the right image. What is important to you? What do you stand for? What are your key messages? What is your "master" skill (the one that differentiates you)? Referring back to a tightly condensed focus sentence is beneficial as you create every new piece of branded marketing material. You will find opportunities to expand on the ideas in this sentence as you develop your digital presence and in your printed promotional material. Known for her sustainable and ethical values, Stella McCartney makes her values clear on her website, and her refusal to use leather or fur is just part of a commitment to leading "a responsible, honest, and modern company" (net-a-porter.com). Her customer will certainly share the same values. From a totally different design perspective, Moschino customers value the brand's unmistakable bold, colorful and whimsical pop culture style.

Analyze your skills and attributes

Create a detailed, prioritized skills list. Understanding is the first step toward visually and verbally articulating what you do best. Ruthlessly evaluate your proficiencies. What are your strengths and weaknesses? How can this be most clearly demonstrated? A skills list supplements your focus sentence, helping you develop and target all your branding material more specifically.

Define your voice

Your style and skills work together intimately to create an overall picture of potential. What do you want people to remember about you? Think about immediate impressions and long-term impact. Your voice should come through in visual, written, and spoken material. Carefully consider what interests, inspires, and motivates your target audience. Where are the intersections between your voice and your audience's needs and desires? As you develop professionally, cultivate and fine tune your voice to make this clear.

(opposite, top) Branded accessories and embellishments from Moschino, F/W 2020 collection.

(opposite bottom) Moschino handbag, S/S 2022 collection.

Create your story

The "story" embedded in every piece of your marketing mix (portfolio, website, résumé, business card, promotional material, and social media presence) is the driving force behind your work. A properly told story enables the viewer to get a comprehensive impression of your style and what motivates you. It is the map leading potential employers toward understanding and appreciating your work.

What is your name?

Will you adopt a professional name? Some designers adopt an alternative name that fits their fashion area and positioning. For instance, Coco Chanel was born Gabrielle Chanel. Sometimes middle names, nicknames, or mother's maiden names take center stage. Alexander McQueen was originally Lee Alexander McQueen. Other designers choose anagrams. Canadian-born American fashion designer Arnold Isaacs reversed the letters of his last name to become Arnold Scaasi.

Be authentic

You should begin to create a genuine connection by demonstrating what really matters to you. People hire people, not just a bundle of skills. When you create an honest story and extend it into multiple formats, you provide insight. Your truth resonates with the viewer.

Engage

You are a storyteller. Just as a movie narrator captures the viewer's interest and helps the story move forward, so a well-crafted personal story based on self-knowledge will capture the interest of potential employers. A properly positioned story functions as a reason for choosing you above the competition.

(opposite, top) Stella McCartney F/W 2020 collection. Referring to the coronavirus pandemic: "Though we are currently facing an unprecedented challenge, there are silver linings like less pollution and more wildlife activity. With our society standing still, we can see for the first time in history our full impact on the planet." Stella McCartney website.

(opposite, below) Stella McCartney F/W 2020 collection.

(right) Céline Haddad, hand-stitched garment label.

Define Your Look

You define a personal visual vocabulary when creating a brand identity system. Portfolio, website, résumé, business card, promotional material, and social media presence are all unified by consistent use of logo, typeface, and layout, Every choice and design element must be in alignment with the impression you want to make. This identity should be flexible enough to be used in a variety of situations but defined enough to be recognizable. We live in a world of information overload, so it is important to make your visual presence arresting as well as easy to understand. An identity system is an aesthetically pleasing demonstration of your communication skills that is meaningful and practical.

Visual elements

Visual brand elements (sometimes called assets) such as logo and font are the building blocks of every piece of marketing material you create. Each element is a clear, targeted signal. Consistent use of the same visual elements throughout your material reinforces specific values and style for the audience. As the graphic designer Paul Rand is often quoted to have said, "Design is the silent ambassador of your brand."

High-quality visuals provide the best impression, so think about hiring professional graphic designers, photographers, or website designers if you do not consider your own skills up to the task.

(below) Hermès signature packaging—boxes and ribbon.

Logo

Every designer should have a simple, easy-to-understand logo. It should capture your style and major attributes, communicating them quickly. This will become a repeatable visual signature. Either a solely typographic approach (logotype) focusing on your name, or a figurative symbol (logomark) may stand alone. Often a standard relationship is established between these, combining name and symbol (combination mark). A logo should be easy to use across various media and at different sizes: personalized stationery, business card, webpage header, and social media sites. It must be clear and legible in both color and black and white. Finding just the right form for your logo takes patient exploration and experimentation. A strong logo embeds itself in audience consciousness, carrying meaning even when viewed alone. Think about the brand marks you immediately recognize, such as Chanel, Apple, and Coca-Cola.

(Below) A logotype and pegasus (winged horse) symbol as a combination mark.

Typeface selection

A typeface that complements your logo will create continuity of meaning across your marketing material. Be sure to make both a logical and intuitive match as you choose this second core communication tool. A typeface must be both adaptable and legible. Commit to just one or two typefaces to support your brand image. Most graphic designers will choose a primary typeface to complement a logo for use in larger size type. A secondary typeface will often be selected for large amounts of smaller text. Different type weights are used as the situation demands. When words in a small-size serif typeface such a Bodoni (with thin serifs) are placed directly on a dark background, the text is best used in a slightly heavier weight to bolster legibility. Investigate and experiment. These choices give nuance and polish to your personal branding.

Most common typefaces are serif or sans serif. Script typefaces are also available. A serif is the small stroke at the end of the main vertical and horizontal strokes of some letters. Any typeface without this detail is referred to as sans serif; common examples are Helvetica and Avenir. These are often chosen to indicate a clean, contemporary style. Use of a serif typeface, like Bodoni, can be suggestive of a more classic style, but there are no hard and fast rules. The type used for headlines and logotypes is referred to as display type. Text typefaces are designed for legibility of continuous text and are generally less overtly distinctive. Script typefaces may be used in display sizes but are rarely used for continuous text. Typeface choice should always help describe the brand's personality. A headline should be clear and impactful. Headline and the text typefaces are always chosen to complement each other, though one may be serif and the other sans serif.

A viewer does not need to be familiar with typefaces to recognize them as part of a brand's visual system. Consumers instantly recognize the BBC logo (in Gill Sans Std) or the Dolce and Gabbana logo, D&G (Futura Demi Bold). Apple has cycled through three similar typefaces during its life. The company's sans-serif font has been continually refined as Apple's minimalistic graphic system and brand image evolve. Today Apple uses a custom sans-serif font called San Francisco, designed in 2017.

Color palette

Color sways opinion. Carefully select a color or colors to serve as a signature for your brand. The elegance of Hermès comes to mind when a certain orange is paired with a deep brown. Select colors that highlight your brand's strengths. You might choose fuchsia as an accent color if marketing directly to preteen girls. Your color choice should evoke intuitive emotional reactions. Together with typeface and logo, color will become one of the most significant elements of your identity system.

Take into account the different associations that colors carry. In many cultures, black represents elegance and simplicity: think little black dress. Depending on the usage, black can also represent mourning and evil. White is associated with minimalism in contemporary graphic design. In the West, white has a historic association with purity, making it popular for wedding gowns, while in some Eastern cultures white can be associated with death. Red is a powerful, emotionally intense color, associated with danger, strength, passion, desire, and love in the West, while in Asian cultures it can represent good fortune and joy.

The consistent use of color increases brand recognition. Your selected colors should be integrated across all material. We associate black and white with all the elements of the Chanel brand. A certain shade of blue evokes Tiffany. Purple sings out Liberty of London, while a particular bright yellow says Selfridges. We have been educated by repeat exposure to immediately understand these colors, the associated company, and the values they represent. So when we see these colors in signage, packaging, or promotional material we understand a great deal in the blink of an eye. Color becomes a long-term asset, so think carefully about the viewer response you want to stimulate. Will the color you choose help a viewer understand your brand as fun or elegant, light and feminine, or bold and minimal?

How do you select the right typeface for your marketing material? When working in Illustrator, take a look at Adobe fonts. Continue your search by investigating open-source font websites such as Dafont or Google Fonts. Open-source typefaces are usually inexpensive or free. However, sometimes it is important to pay for just the right font, in which case browse FontFont, FontShop, or MyFonts. You will find a huge choice. Clean, simple typefaces are most adaptable to different situations. A few classic typefaces that often work well are Gill Sans (sans serif), Caslon (serif), and Didot (serif).

(above) Fashion magazine logos based on the versatile Didot typeface, *Elle* and *Harper's Bazaar*.

(above) Standard Tiffany packaging in signature robin's egg blue with white satin ribbon.

A few practical notes: don't forget the functional legibility of dark colored type on a light background, and the importance of a harmonious relationship between any of the colors you choose to represent the brand. For a powerful, bold impact, contrasting complementary colors work well together: black and white, red and grccn, orange and blue, yellow and purple. Another approach is to use gradients of colors with variations in saturation to build an array of tones supporting specific looks or themes A selected palette is integral in translating a designer's concept. To prevent predictability and ensure freshness, mix in one or two accent colors. Shipping giant FedEx always uses their base purple for the Fed portion of the logo. A different primary color is used on the Ex portion of the logo to signal different business functions within the company. These choices bring increased clarity to corporate communication.

(above, left to right) Olga Singh and Céline Haddad, headshots used for promotion and on social media.

(opposite) SeungYeon Kim, Packaged to Go collection unit (capsule collection). Consistent digital presentation in research, technical sketches, process, and finished garment.

Photographs and headshots

Photographic style speaks volumes. The photographic representation of your fashion product should embody your overall style just as eloquently as it captures the collection attitude.

Consider carefully: does your budget allow for a professional or will you be able to recruit the help of a friend who is talented with a camera? Is a soft or sharp focus image more appropriate? Do you prefer color or black-and-white photography? Will the lighting be strong and direct or softly atmospheric? How will you style the product? For inspiration look at the work of fashion photographers such as Deborah Turbeville, Steven Meisel, Herb Ritts, Juergen Teller, and Arthur Elgort.

Create a consistent headshot of yourself to serve as a signature image on your website and social media channels. Think carefully about how this image is reflective of your personal brand.

Applying Branding to Media

Be judicious in your selection of printed and digital media, as well as in the application of your personal brand image. Make social media and web choices based on your audience, needs, and projected impact. Reinforce your core messaging with recurring use of typefaces, colors, and images. While application can vary, use of these elements must always remain true to the core look and values established in your personal brand strategy and identity.

Portfolio

As you prepare your portfolio, take into account the overall visual attitude of your brand identity. In both an analog and digital portfolio, the introductory page should focus on your logo. Following pages should reinforce the narrative of the overall portfolio with consistent formatting and type. You may develop a unique presentation format for capsule collections or specific studies.

TECHNICAL BINDER
SeungYeon Kim

PACKAGED TO GO
Seungyeon Kim

PAPER BAG + SHIRT
DRESS

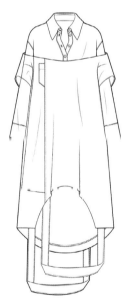

BONDED COTTON   COTTON POPLIN   CLUSTER BEADING   LAMBSKIN

Business card

A business card is a conceptual reminder and factual document. Make sure your card does both jobs well. The standard information provided on a business card is name, address, phone number, email, and website. You may choose to leave out the address or add dedicated social media accounts such as Twitter or Instagram. The card itself should be physically small, fitting easily into a standard wallet, but should not be so small that it can be easily lost. A typical US business card size is 2 x 3½ inches (in Europe it is generally 55 x 85 mm). It could be used in either portrait (vertical) or landscape (horizontal) orientation, and it may be printed on both or only one side. These specifications are not set in stone, they may vary to satisfy your brand's distinctive style.

In laying out the visual elements of your personal brand on the card, pay attention to choice of image, legibility, visual organization, and information hierarchy. For example, your name is often more visually important than the address, email, and phone number. There should be an overall professional sophistication to your approach; business cards are tactile marketing tools meant to be passed from one person to another. Interesting visual details and paper choice add a memorable professional touch. When you are not present, make sure this physically small piece of branding represents you beautifully and clearly.

Choosing a substantial paper projects quality. Online printers such as MOO and 4x6 offer a selection of papers and finishes at very reasonable prices. Paper is referred to as "stock" and your choice should feel rigid in the hand. 14- or 16-point card stock are common choices. If you want extra thick cards choose 18- or 32-point stock.

Paper choice represents your brand as strongly as graphics or words. The most common finishes are dull matte, satin, and glossy. Textured or specialty papers (such as metallics) are often available. Paper may be coated or uncoated: coated paper has a protective finish and typically produces a sharper, cleaner printed image. Select shape, size, card stock, color, texture, and text to present the image that best sums up your style. For example, consider using recycled paper if sustainability is important to your brand.

(opposite) Man Yan, promotional card front and back with traditional Chinese identification stamp.

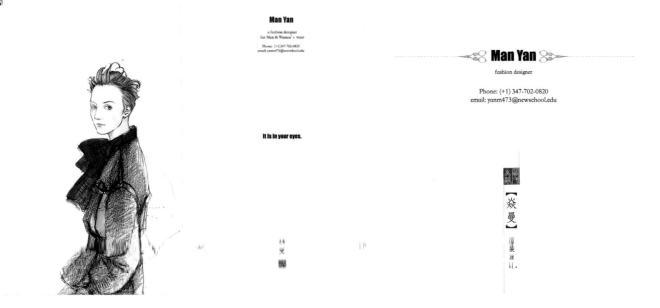

(opposite) Mengyao Xiong, boxed set of promotional cards.

(above) Mengyao Xiong, one of a series of promotional cards paired with business card, front and back.

(left) Rich Daniel, one of a series of promotional cards paired with business card.

Résumé

The résumé or CV (curriculum vitae) is a basic job search tool. It introduces the jobseeker to the potential employer. This document is one or two pages detailing your aims, skills, education, jobs, and significant accomplishments. Visually it is directly related to your business card design. A journalist seeking a position with a fashion magazine may be asked for an expanded document listing prior published articles. In academia, a CV is an expanded multipage document detailing all academic accomplishments and published material. For the fashion industry, core data about potential candidates is supplied by standard résumés.

Keep the information on your résumé brief. Remember it is a snapshot, not a biography. It is especially important that the typeface is clean, simple, and legible. Lay out the document for both legibility and style—many templates are available online. A résumé demonstrates your ability to skillfully write, organize, and communicate. Thoughtful coordination of itemized facts should combine with your targeted visual brand image. Create a powerful career statement with use of your logo as well as consistent typefaces and layout style. For all interviews, have a few copies of your printed résumé with you. It is a good idea to have a digital version of your résumé available for electronic communication.

There are two main types of résumé: chronological and functional. The more familiar chronological résumé is a list of work experience in reverse chronological order (beginning with the most recent). The functional résumé starts with your achievements and skills, moving on to your work history later. Experiment with a combination of formats until you find the best balance to represent your particular attributes, skills, and background. This combination document will become the basic résumé that you custom tailor for each interview.

As you get ready to apply for each job you will be creating targeted combination résumés. As you customize your basic résumé toward the needs and interests of a specific employer, it could mean changing the skill sets highlighted or tweaking your summary. Be flexible.

Although the core content of the résumé is similar for most parts of the world, there may be slight differences. For instance, in some countries it is customary to include date of birth, headshot, or citizenship. It is unusual to include these in a document targeted for US or UK employment. When preparing a résumé, be guided by résumé samples originating from the country where the job is located or the hiring is happening.

The following sections are organized with recent graduates in mind. As you gain more experience, the order may change. This combination format marries the best aspects of a chronological résumé and a functional résumé. It uses both work history and skills to capture the employer's attention.

Contact information

Summary

Education

Work experience

Skills

Contact information

This is the most important part of your résumé. It is how an interested employer reaches you. Clearly include your name, local address (at least your city and state/county), phone number, email address, and website. Some choose to omit the street address, but be sure to provide the widest opportunity for potential employers to contact you.

Summary

This should be no more than a few sentences. Even an entry-level applicant can use this section to briefly and concisely describe their career goals. Later in your career this will be the place where you describe how your skills and experience meet the needs of the job. You might call this either qualifications or summary.

Education

Simply state your degree/s and your university name, location, and dates of study. If you had a particular accomplishment in your educational experience, such as foreign study, add this.

Work experience

List the names and location of former employers, beginning with the most recent and working back. Add your title and responsibilities as well as dates of employment. An entry-level applicant may include non-fashion-related positions, part-time work, and internships.

Skills

Include a list of 5–10 of your strongest skills. This is a list of the abilities that make you an attractive candidate. Specifically curate your choices to make them appropriate for the job you are applying for,

Optional sections

Depending on your background you may choose to add sections for publications, awards, languages, and associations.

Larger companies will often use an applicant tracking system (ATS) to cull résumés and cover letters. This software will search by keyword and other criteria, then save the information to a database. For this reason, make sure you have embedded pertinent keywords in your résumé. It can be tricky to create a readable informational document for humans with this type of machine search in mind. The very specific wording in a job posting is your best guide. Be careful with acronyms; include both the abbreviation and the full name. Use full numbers for years (so "2022" not "22") and emphasize hard skills such as patternmaking and technical drawing. Your aim is to get your résumé past the automated programmed search and into human hands.

WilliamHarris

10 Anyplace Ave New York, New York 12345 Williamharris@gmail.com Williamharris.com 212 654 1234

Dear *Hiring manager's name*,

Lorem ipsum dolor sit amet, consectetur adipiscing elit. Fusce iaculis vel neque at suscipit. Ut a augue risus. Maecenas semper dolor velit, nec tincidunt massa rutrum sit amet. Praesent ut enim sed purus pretium tempus. Suspendisse ipsum urna, pharetra non bibendum id, fermentum ut libero. Nulla facilisi. Fusce nec orci et tortor blandit pulvinar vitae id urna. Fusce vehicula vel nibh ac feugiat. Ut consectetur felis ac tellus tincidunt, non cursus diam eleifend. Nam mattis nibh ante, non aliquet nisl commodo vitae. Pellentesque quis tellus mattis, accumsan urna sit amet, placerat mi. Donec congue mi tincidunt augue imperdiet maximus. Orci varius natoque penatibus et magnis dis parturient montes, nascetur ridiculus mus. Mauris ullamcorper tempor cursus. Donec at eros convallis, suscipit libero ut, placerat sem. Donec malesuada commodo lorem eget tincidunt

Pellentesque porta iaculis sem at tincidunt.
Class aptent taciti sociosqu ad litora torquent per conubia nostra, per inceptos himenaeos.

Sincerely,

William Harris

VALENTINA RICCI

v.ricci@gmail.com | 01234 123456 | valentinaricci.com

Dear Ola Schmid

Consectetur adipiscing elit. Suspendisse sollicitudin sapien at neque gravida, id varius diam efficitur. Integer eu felis vitae justo sagittis pretium. Etiam lacinia leo eget lacus imperdiet, sod dignissim orci lobortis. In in felis urna. Sed tortor tellus, rutrum sed vehicula vel, dapibus Vestibulum mollis lectus ut cursus vestibulum. Nam accumsan nisi diam, in consequat leo pretium suscipit. Nunc pretium dapibus lacinia. Suspendisse non metus augue.

Nunc laoreet ut ligula sed molestie. Nullam ultricies purus quis ligula dignissim rhoncus. Duis interdum sollicitudin ligula ac vehicula. Vivamus ullamcorper vitae enim et lobortis. Etiam ultrices arcu vitae sapien lobortis luctus. Proin in mattis turpis, quis posuere elit. Nullam in lobortis urna, at auctor magna. Curabitur a tellus sit amet ligula congue sagittis eget vitae risus. Fusce commodo eget elit in sollicitudin.

Nam dignissim efficitur lacus vitae ultricies. Quisque eget est malesuada, interdum ante vitae, porttitor quam. Suspendisse commodo convallis placerat. Integer gravida metus in vestibulum volutpat. Pellentesque ac faucibus ex. Pellentesque commodo imperdiet pellentesque. Donec at et malesuada fames ac turpis egestas. Integer pellentesque neque sed convallis varius.

Pellentesque ultrices ligula a est tempus bibendum. Sed gravida porta ligula nec vehicula.

Sincerely,
Valentina Ricci

WilliamHarris

10 Anyplace Ave New York, New York 12345 Williamharris@gmail.com Williamharris.com 212 654 1234

Objective
High energy women's apparel designer
seeking associate position with opportunity for broad learning, technical skill
development and advancement.

Skills
Structural design and construction techniques
Colorways and color stories
Hand and digital flats
Material and trim research
Market and trend research
Attention to detail
Organized mult-itasker
Works well under pressure
Collaborative
Adaptable
Fluent Spanish

Digital Skills
Adobe Photoshop and Illustrator, Kaledo
Microsoft Word, and Excel

Experience
Daisy and Rose
Assistant designer - Juniors - Jan 2019 - Current
Involved in all aspects of design and product development, Assisted head designer on the
design of private label dresses for Kohls and Forever 21: preparing first samples, follow up on
lab-dip and strike-off approvals and samples. Attended fit sessions to review overall silhouette
and execution of garments. Created seasonal color palettes. Formulated and structured costing
charts. Organized and compiled samples for line review presentations, internal use
and advertising and PR shoots.

Baby Brew Streetwear
Intern - Oct - Dec 2018
Created seasonal color palettes and developed colorways. Created digital flats in
Illustrator. Formulated and organized costing chart
In charge of sample room inventory. Developed and tracked sample spec sheet.

Denim Doll
Intern - Jan - April 2017
Researched trends. Formulated and structured costing charts
Organized archives. Created moodboards. Sourced trim

Volunteer Work
New York Fashion Week -- September 2016
Dresser for Yeoh Lee's Spring Summer Collection Fashion Show

Education
Bachelor of Fine Arts - May 2017
Fashion Design
Fashion Institute of Technology State University of New York
Deans' List

VALENTINA RICCI

v.ricci@gmail.com | 01234 123456 | valentinaricci.com

SUMMARY
Intimate Apparel designer seeking challenging position with opportunity for broad
learning and further technical skill development

WORK HISTORY

Designer Merchandiser—Intimate Apparel   August 2021-Current
Crush
- Designed private label sleepwear annd lingerie, interfaced with overseas factories
- Sourced and developed new trims and laces
- Worked with technical designers to created specs for new bodies
- Organized and formulated costing charts
- Created line catalogues

Associate Designer— Intimate Apparel   January 2019-August 2021
Softwear
- Designed women's sleepwear
- Developed digital flats and spec sheets
- Maintained technical sketch library
- Created seasonal color palettes
- Organized and formuated costing charts
- Designed/merchandised showroom for market week

Associate Designer—Swimwear   February 2018-January 2019
LA Swimwear
- Designed junior swimwear
- Attended fit sessions to review overall silhouette and execution of garments
- Created seasonal color palettes
- Organized and compiled samples for line review presentation and photoshoots
- In charge of sample room inventory

Associate Designer—Sleepwear   February 2017-February 2018
Bloom
- Assisted with private label sleepwear designs
- Reviewed and approved Lab dips and strike-offs
- Sourced prints and created colorways in Adobe Photoshop
- Created detailed flats under the guidance of the head designer
- Assisted the technical designer and patternmaker

EDUCATION
BA (Hons) Fashion—Fashion Design Womenswear   May 2016
Chelsea College of Art and Design

Foundation Diploma in Art and Design   May 2012
London College of Fashion

Cover letter

When a résumé is submitted it is accompanied by a cover letter that focuses on providing the reader with specific reasons for serious consideration of your application. Graphically, the letter style and typeface should match your résumé. The letter should highlight your most relevant qualifications as well as providing insight into your soft skills (i.e. organization and active listening), attitude, and motivations. An employer should get a sense of an applicant's ability to adapt to company culture and accomplish job requirements. If submitting a résumé by email, make sure to provide cover letter information within the text of the email.

Promotional email

Since a large portion of adults have an email account, email promotion with broad and direct reach should be used to complement chosen social media platforms. Not all clients will use all social media platforms and not all content is relevant to all clients or search situations. Tailor the content of your email (written presentation of your skills and visual material) to the particular opportunities. Always use a graphic format that includes as many of the visual elements of your personal brand as possible: logo, typeface, color, and layout style. You may choose to create a custom signature for emails within the body of your email.

When creating a business email address, make it professional and relatively easy to remember. Your first and last name is the most memorable and direct choice.

Look-book and line-sheet as marketing tools

The look-book is a marketing tool that should provide both inspiration and information to the viewer. It is essentially a collection of photographs of garments or other fashion product, styled to show brand and collection content and style while specifically demonstrating material and construction detail. The clothing is the star. For a consumer, a look-book may serve as a fashion style-guide showing how garments should be worn. A line-sheet is a functional document used in the ordering process. For the retail buyer, it is an informational catalog for assortment selection. A look-book is a time-consuming but valuable endeavor. Depending on finance and market conditions you may choose a printed look-book, a digital look-book, or simply a line-sheet.

Package your look-book with an arresting cover that relates to the content and is directly on strategy. If there is an especially important design detail, include close-ups. Choose 30–60 words to describe each collection or curated group of designs. When laying the book out, remember the importance of image and page sequence (see p.65).

The line-sheet is composed of line drawings or photographs of garments on a flat surface. Garments are described by SKU (stock keeping unit), colors, fabrics, sizes, the wholesale price (without VAT), and the recommended retail price.

(opposite, top) Cover letters matching your graphic system highlight specific qualifications and notable skills. (The text used in the examples is dummy text.)

(opposite, below) Résumés are designed to match your graphic system. They organize job qualifications and give a sense of applicant style. (The text used in the examples is dummy text.)

(over the page) Céline Haddad, look-book pages, Rebellion Collection 1.

16 . 17

6 . 7

20 . 21

52 . 53

Website

This is your online home base. Make sure to give clear prominence to your logo for both personal sites and umbrella sites (see p.92).

In website design, utility trumps aesthetics. Select menu sections carefully and make sure images load quickly. Use the same typeface you have chosen for other marketing materials in order to maintain a consistent style and image. If your typeface is not web accessible for bulk text or menu usage, make a choice as close in style as possible.

Your website address is an important decision as you will live with it for a long time. Follow the same rule as for your professional email address—in most cases this will mean basing it on your first and last name or your registered corporate name.

Regularly update your website with new work.

(above) Céline Haddad, website pages viewed on a desktop monitor.

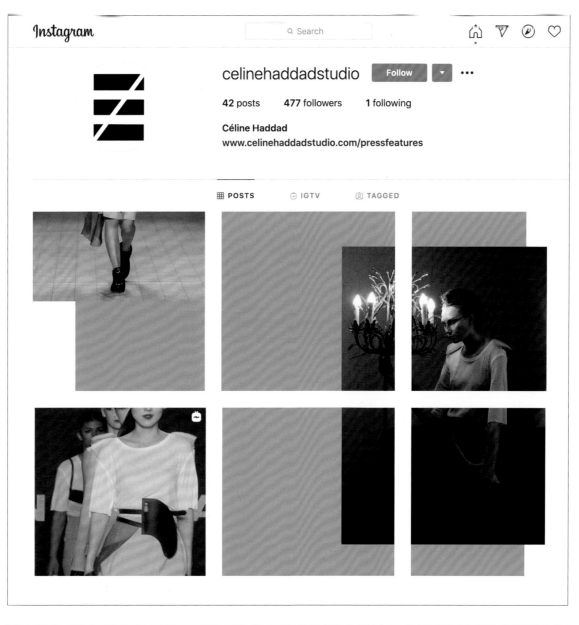

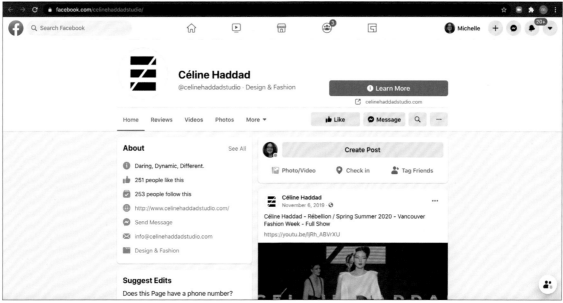

Social media

Social media, whether it is LinkedIn, Twitter, or Instagram, embodies your voice and values in tone, image, and words. Pay particular attention to LinkedIn and Instagram as they are often relied upon by recruiters as primary background resources.

Utilize the same profile photo and common cover images across social media channels to boost immediate recognition and reinforce your brand. Whenever possible, add your logo and utilize your brand colors and fonts. It is important to make sure that your logo design works well in the formats of your chosen social media sites.

Optimize your social media presence with a strong combination of visual attitude and content. Everything must work together seamlessly and resonate with your audience. Remove any unflattering or distracting personal images from social media. Think about what content you can post that will reinforce your overall concept. Do you have new work to show? Has your work been featured in a magazine, website, or fashion show?

Work identification

Any freelance work turned in to a client is a marketing opportunity. Clearly and unobtrusively brand your work with your name, contact information, and logo. This may result in more work at a later date.

Email signature

A clear, informative signature should conclude every email. Include: your full name, email address, telephone number, logo, and company name as well as icons for brand-linked social media.

(opposite) Céline Haddad, Instagram and Facebook pages featuring Rebellion Collection 1, Vancouver Fashion Week.

NIMBUS

Yuhan Bi
biy167@newschool.edu

Review

Storytelling matters. Personal branding is both an art and a science. Involving potential employers in your story via a personal brand strategy increases your chances for a connection and then an opportunity. The unique tone and style you develop should be carried through all of your marketing materials.

Consistent use of core visual elements supporting a personal brand strategy reinforces meaning and educates the viewer as to designer proficiencies and aesthetics.

Pay careful attention to consistent use of logo brand colors and signature typefaces in portfolio, résumé, business card, look-book, line-sheet, social media, and any other marketing material. Photography should always be consistent and express brand attitude.

Your personal brand story is a promise. It speaks of your skills, attitudes, and what can be expected. It hints at what can be accomplished.

Dos and Don'ts

Do create a strong personal brand strategy based on your skill set, attitude, and attributes

Don't deviate from this strategy in any materials connected to your job search

Do seek to engage your target audience with a well-crafted, consistent story

Don't forget this story is represented in writing as well as visually and verbally

Do think of your personal brand design as a visual representation of the meaning embedded in your brand strategy

Don't forget to focus on making an emotional connection

Do develop a look-book containing a few of your most relevant designs

Don't make your look-book into a mini portfolio

Do remember that your core visual elements may be modified based on media, but not significantly altered

Don't forget that consistency reinforces understanding and optimizes chances for success

Quick Quiz

- What are the six areas of focus in developing a personal brand strategy?

- What are the core visual components of a personal brand?

- What are the most important things to pay attention to when designing a business card?

- Which social media platforms are most often used as a background checking resource by recruiters?

(opposite) Yuhan Bi, promotional cards featuring a scope of work, shown with business card.

CHAPTER 5

Social Media and Self-promotion

The Key Channels
Building a Social Media Following
Self-promotion

Today you cannot have a fashion career without a social media presence. To build the right traction and momentum means evaluating multiple channels and choosing those that fit your style, voice, and target audience. While there is no one-size-fits-all solution, Instagram and Twitter have become global communication standards. For the right designer, Pinterest is also a smart channel choice. Snapchat or TikTok are most appropriate for particular demographics. When deciding which social media channels to prioritize, keep your eyes open for developing apps and user trends.

The Key Channels

Monitoring the current climate is essential when you are researching social media channels. Social media rules are constantly changing as commercial and legal issues continue to modify the landscape. New platforms are continuously developing. Social networking platforms frequently tweak the algorithms that determine what surfaces in users' feeds. Existing platforms take on new roles. Where one channel might have once led, it could be in decline or no longer used by your target demographic. Keep posted.

Benefits of a Social Media Presence

- Increased brand awareness
- Immediate customer connection
- Direct customer feedback
- Unsolicited customer testimonials
- Customer-based inspiration
- Discovering/promoting collaborations
- Easy and immediate presentation of new concepts
- Improved brand authority
- Traffic directed to your website
- Building a loyal set of followers

(below) Social media symbols: Instagram, Facebook, Twitter, Pinterest; YouTube, TikTok, Snapchat, LinkedIn.

Instagram

A highly visual, continually growing platform with well over a billion followers, this app accounts for a very large percentage of brand posts. Instagram allows the owner to carefully curate content, encourages user-generated material, and provides powerful storytelling capability. It often allows followers an intimate peek behind the scenes,

Instagram Stories (like Snapchat) last a maximum of 24 hours. For those who are already creating product, you may choose to make your feed shoppable. Instagram is a great way to partner with influencers; a correctly selected influencer helps boost trust and promotes content to the right audience. Viewed as the most visual of the popular platforms, here "A picture is worth a thousand words". Ensure you provide beautiful, well-styled, high-resolution images that tell the right story.

To become reachable, organize communication around your brand's hashtag. Think about creating an online event. Encourage people to post multiple kinds of media files. This stimulates added viewer interest.

Facebook

Even with the continuing evolution of customer use times and demographics, this platform remains powerful in creating fashion-related conversations and connections. Understand your customer and be specific when targeting age or lifestyle groups. Zero in on your specific niche. Focus on engagement and customer relationship management more than commerce. Most people choose to visit a Facebook page to learn more about the personality of a brand rather than to directly shop. Humanize your content. Make it entertaining, inviting, and intimate.

Twitter

Twitter is more than just a few words. It is a targeted way to get your brand noticed using images and up to 280 well-chosen characters. It is about immediacy and brevity.

Be aware of what the competition is doing. As you become familiar with Twitter's tools, investigate, analyze, and expand how you use the platform.

Selection of available tools:

- TweetDeck
- Hootsuite
- bit.ly
- Agorapulse
- Buffer

Pinterest

A powerful and visually engaging tool to reach new customers, Pinterest has a smaller customer base than Instagram. These customers look for ideas and inspiration, not brands. Because most searches are about discovery, a small brand or designer has a good opportunity to engage the right consumers. Clearly organize your content for maximum impact. Make discovery and wandering easy. Optimize your pins for discovery with strong keywords and detailed descriptions of products. As always, photos should be carefully curated and high resolution. As with Instagram and Twitter, stay on-brand and make sure to create effective narratives with your choices.

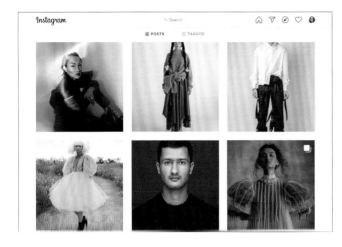

(left) Ikshit Pande, QUOD on Instagram.

(below) 0.5 Olga Singh on Facebook.

(bottom) Joan Dominique, Pinterest cross-promotion of makeup and footwear.

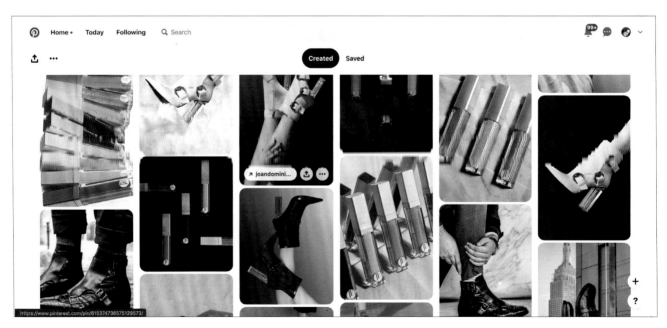

YouTube

Movement motivates. YouTube can be a cost-effective way to distribute video content. It is both a social platform and a search engine, so title your videos in ways that are both descriptive and desirable. Create clear thumbnails as well as a complete and informative About section. This is an ideal place to post supplementary material in a motion format. You may want to play around with the Google Keyword Optimizer. As with everything in social media, it is vital to be directly responsive. Build interactivity by asking for comments and shares. Create content based on feedback. Develop creative contests to engage existing followers and build new ones. Provide a look behind the scenes of fashion shows or product development. Followers love to see behind the curtain. Ask viewers to subscribe to your channel and recommend your videos: by allowing people to share and embed they participate in your story. As subscriber and recommendation count grows, you will increase your views and overall visibility.

TikTok

Popular in China since 2016, and seeing growth after it became available worldwide in 2018, TikTok provides a home for videos under 60 seconds long. It syncs well with short attention spans, making it a useful tool for designers targeting Gen Z. The platform is an inviting space for self-expression and a good home for candid unfiltered content. TikTok's audience responds to challenges and contests. "Through the Decades" challenges TikTokers to explore their own take on the fashion aesthetics of different eras. In the Guess-sponsored "In my Denim" challenge, TikTokers go from disheveled to glamorous. After looks feature Guess product. Millions of fans experiment with their own versions of the transformation. TikTok creativity will continue to mirror developments in the fashion industry and reflect changing generational tastes.

Snapchat

Tailored for a mobile-first generation, Snapchat's demographic leans slightly older than TikTok's, including more Millennials. The platform is about capturing the moment, with features that allow easy and quick editing of pictures and videos. Filters add to the immediate creativity and excitement of content that self-destroys in 24 hours. The instant nature of the content makes interaction more intimate. A brand can become part of users' everyday interactions. Effective advertising on Snapchat is expensive and may not fit your budget. Research cost carefully

LinkedIn

Originally conceived as a job search tool, LinkedIn has grown and expanded into a major networking website. Currently, setting up and maintaining a profile allows you to build and manage your network, as well as curate the presentation of a professional identity. By linking your website, posting your résumé, and writing articles you can grow awareness of your brand as well as develop connections for freelance work or full-time work.

(top) Céline Haddad fashion show, Vancouver Fashion Week, on YouTube.

(above) Ikshit Pande, QUOD NYC, S/S 2021 collection on LinkedIn.

Building a Social Media Following

Your presence on social media should be defined by consistent style in visuals, motion, and written content. You have crafted a strong identity: reinforce it whenever possible. All material presented on your social media accounts should be cohesive and on-brand. The voice established in your personal brand strategy should be clearly evident as you share only focused, high-quality content.

Image

Since fashion is a visual field, your statement needs to start with the look of your profile. You are the face of your brand. Build around a signature profile picture that captures the brand essence. This should be consistent on all platforms. For Twitter, both your display and cover pictures must be captivating and on-brand. These will nonverbally speak for you. On some platforms you may choose to add a logo. Where necessary, support product imagery with brief, one-line descriptions.

Text

Your bio should be short, snappy, clear, and engaging—as well as consistent across platforms. All profiles should include a link to your website. Written content, whether in your profile or posted, should be crisp, easily understandable, and proofread. Write in a manner that reflects your brand strategy in both spirit and style.

Followers

Social media success is about earning attention by nurturing relationships. Followers are without doubt the key to effective social media. Bond with them and inspire passion. Building a substantial following requires an investment of time and effort. Do the research, check out competitors, and seek active interest. You want followers who like, comment, share, and engage with your posts. It is about reciprocity. An audience that talks and reacts extends your reach. Like and react to their posts, ask questions, and build a conversation. Make followers part of your story. Unlike a standard advertising campaign this is not just selling, it is sharing. Followers love the idea that their original content may be reposted by a brand and offered to a greater audience.

Authenticity is key with followers. Moments that feel real and genuine give a sense of privilege and intimacy. As a community, consumers are hypersensitive to insincerity and lack of authenticity. They tend to generously share both positive and negative reactions.

Hashtags

Hashtags are a way to connect social media to a specific searchable theme, event, or conversation. If you want to be noticed and build a following, make sure the hashtags you choose are not so specific as to be unsearched, or so general that you will get lost in a sea of similarity. Focus on using no more than 10–15 hashtags. Tag your location for a chance to be featured on location-based stories and pages or use hashtags with the location included. Learning how to monitor hashtag performance can deliver insights about your viewers and provide inspiration. Effective use of hashtags boosts your overall social media engagement.

Working with social media influencers

Building a relationship with the right micro-influencers (fewer than 100,000 followers) will help build brand credibility and create increased engagement. It is best to select a few people with followings that match your targeted demographic. Carefully evaluate voice as well as follower base to align with your values. Building an influencer relationship is slow, progressive work but pays big dividends over time. Remember it is a two-way street—the relationships an influencer builds with the right designers help build their own brand.

(top and above) Influencers promote product with their unique look and styling

Self-promotion

You want to attract attention. In the words of the showman P.T. Barnum: "Without promotion, something terrible happens—nothing." Be patiently, politely persistent. Promoting your goals and accomplishments goes beyond creating a standout portfolio and developing a strong personal branding and social media presence.

In-person communication

Be empathetic. Don't talk *to* an audience, talk *with* them. Listen carefully. Clearly and without pretension, stay on message. Be aware of the listener. Look closely at what you see. Is it boredom, involvement, or distraction? Be interesting and interact. Have an "elevator pitch" ready; this is a very brief, condensed version of your story (no more than 30 seconds). You should know it cold so you can tailor it on the fly to fit circumstances. Be energetic and show passion. Here is an example of an elevator pitch: "Why is most women's lingerie designed for men? I am an intimate apparel designer creating beautiful garments to enhance a woman's spirit and confidence. A woman deserves to appreciate her own body, whatever her shape. I seek an entry-level position in a small luxury brand."

Help other talented individuals. There is value in being visible and creating your own network. This enhances your credibility and encourages others to help and connect you to new resources.

Online presence

Potential employers will be checking on you. Before you start applying for jobs take a look at what will come up on a Google search. As much as possible, clean out any unprofessional materials that could cause concern. Perhaps it's time to remove that picture you took at a topless beach in Antigua from your Facebook page.

Make your professional accomplishments public, especially on LinkedIn, Instagram, and Twitter. Polish your online presence and leverage the special strengths of each channel. Be strategic about your postings. If your work has been featured in a publication or fashion show, let the world know by posting a link, image, or video. Consider writing short articles for LinkedIn. Social media is based on sharing and discovery: the more information and interesting images you provide, the more viewers return. Keep your website updated to reflect those accomplishments.

(above) Stefan Radulescu on Instagram. Self-promotion using social media.

DJIUN

SENIOR DESIGNER
VMAGAZINE & VMAN — COVER DESIGN

More Tweets

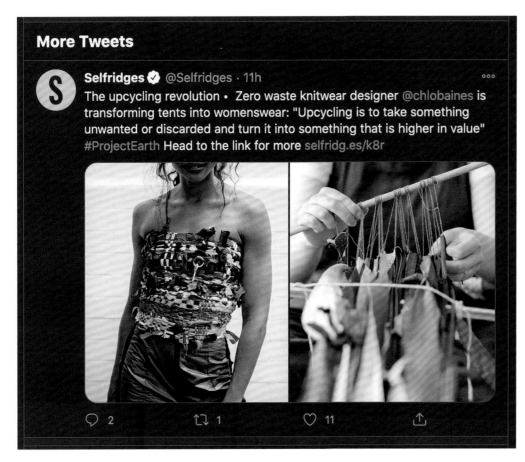

Email and follow-up

Email can be a very targeted personal approach. Focus on one key strategy point when you email useful contacts. Request a result such as a phone call, interview, or email response. Ask for referrals and recommendations as appropriate. Provide well-formatted contact information in the form of an email signature.

If you are reaching out to someone you do not know, you can add a sample or two to provide a flavor of your work. Following up on an interview could mean sending a multipage or a single-page PDF document formatted to match your visual identity. Never forget the power of an old-fashioned thank you. Email is an immediate way to acknowledge those who have helped you. A handwritten note shows a personal touch that is often forgotten in contemporary society.

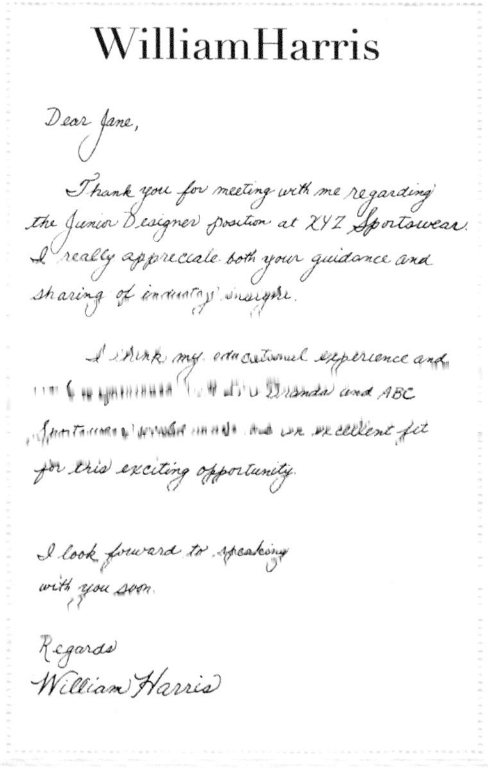

WilliamHarris

Dear Jane,

Thank you for meeting with me regarding the Junior Designer position at XYZ Sportswear. I really appreciate both your guidance and sharing of industry insights.

I think my educational experience and ... Brandex and ABC Sportswear ... an excellent fit for this exciting opportunity.

I look forward to speaking with you soon.

Regards
William Harris

(opposite, top) Djiun Wang cross-promotes his skills as an art director, photographer, and stylist by using a single PDF page of his work as an interview follow-up.

(opposite, below) Selfridges speaks eloquently to its customers on multiple social media platforms.

(right) A hand touch is always appreciated. Carefully select stationery and thoughtfully craft your message when writing to follow up on an interview.

Blogging and content writing

The written word is another way to define your business and yourself. By adding a blog section to your website or creating your own separate blogging site you can clearly allow your personality and opinions to shine through. Like any other interactive social media, a blog supports engagement and makes relationships more personal by encouraging two-way conversations. On a website this can make a great counterpoint to pure commerce.

If writing is a strength of yours, volunteer to write for publications to demonstrate both your communication and fashion skills. Choose to pitch appropriate lifestyle and fashion blogs, websites, or magazines. Both print and online magazines may require proposals and provide specific guidelines.

Blogging continues to evolve as social media usage shifts. As bloggers gain followers, some become influencers. Many choose Instagram or YouTube to offer their perspective. Fashion bloggers often set trends as they follow their passion, sharing knowledge and news. Influencers may photograph or film themselves wearing or demonstrating product. From street wear to fashion shows, blogging or vlogging (video blogging) allows niche ideas and perspectives to take center stage in a global arena.

(opposite) Bloggers filming themselves as well as the styles and trends they want to share.

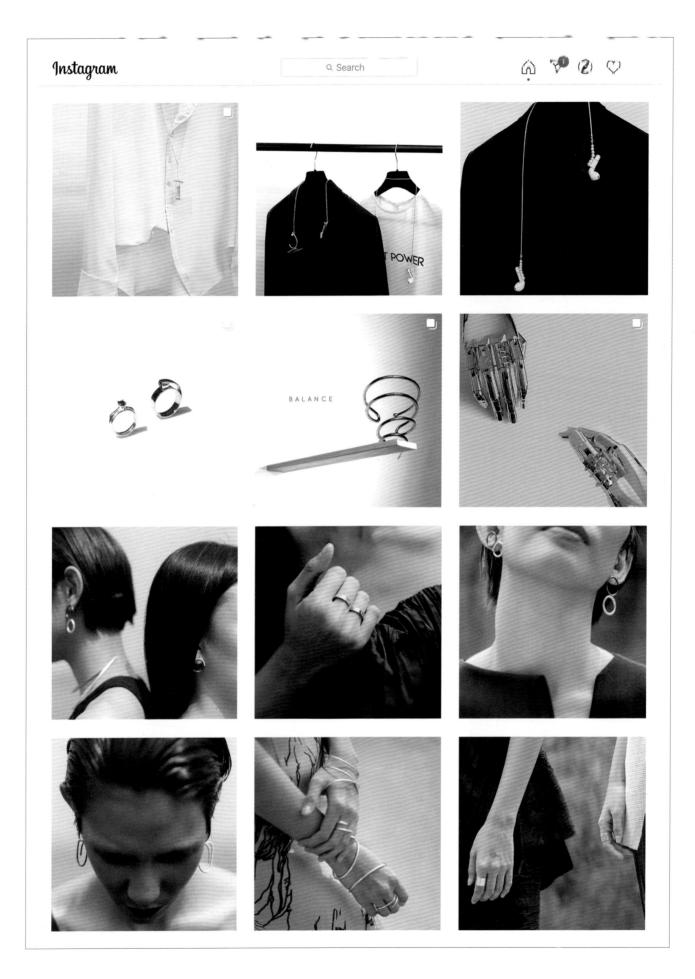

Review

Creative use of social media is about connection and relationships. It focuses on imagery and ideas before sales. From your initial brand strategy, develop a personal social media strategy. Stay fresh and immediate as well as consistent in your communication. Speak directly to your target audience. Use influencers to extend your brand reach.

In utilizing appropriate social media platforms, keep followers curious and hungry. This is a seduction and a friendship. The right content keeps your followers returning for more.

Remain aware of evolving social media trends that you can adapt to your audience. Regularly respond directly to follower posts. Write articles, share events, and make your audience feel intimately involved.

Cross-promote your website, Instagram, Facebook, YouTube, Twitter, Pinterest, or any other platforms you choose. Social media thrives on community, bonding, and sharing.

Dos and Don'ts

Do create a strong, targeted, strategic approach to your social media presence

Don't feel you must be on every available social media platform

Do include Twitter, Instagram, and LinkedIn in your strategy

Don't upload any material not consistent with your overall brand concept

Do shoot a consistent profile picture and create a bio that you use across platforms

Don't ever provide pixelated or visibly low-resolution images

Do select images you can use across multiple launch pages

Don't be inauthentic or inconsistent in your messaging with followers

Quick Quiz

- How do you build an online community?
- How do you select the social media most appropriate for your target audience?
- What kind of material is most appropriate for each social media platform?
- What is the best way to make use of a social influencer?
- In what significant ways can in-person interaction complement social media?

(opposite) Agatha Agatha, RACCOONANDBABIES, Instagram.

Career Paths and Interviews

You have now developed a personal brand strategy and created an image to support it. Your portfolio coordinates beautifully with your social media presence and résumé. In this chapter, as you work toward a productive job search, you will develop your long- and short-term goals. We provide guidance as you discover fashion career paths to further explore.

General information on how to job search is abundant, and Google will direct you to many sites specializing in search advice. However, while there are some fundamental rules that apply to all professions, it is important to do specific job search planning that relates to fashion. Once you have located the right opportunities this will mean reviewing and polishing your résumé as well as networking and exploring recruitment agencies. When you hear back from a potential employer, the interview is the next crucial step, and in order to succeed focused interview planning is necessary.

Fashion Careers

In order to reach your career goals, set clear and specific targets. Do some research on available positions in specific categories and growing disciplines. Are you interested in the creation of garment concepts as a fashion designer, or would you prefer to share your knowledge as a fashion influencer or journalist? Spend time learning what is required to be successful in these positions. Decide on the particular areas of fashion you want to pursue. If you are technically oriented, you might choose the precision of patternmaking. An interest in the performing arts might lead you to costume design. Once again, objectively analyze your strengths, aesthetic perspective, and skills. Do they match the requirements for your field of interest? Is your personality suited to the demands of your chosen discipline?

The fashion industry offers a wide array of opportunities for the talented and skilled. Some are more creative; others are related to the product production process and are more technical. The fashion design portfolio can become a gateway to opportunities in fashion design, patternmaking, and costume design. Creative interests can also be channeled into media. The worlds of online and print fashion journalism, photography, and styling have been joined by the quickly evolving field of fashion influencers. A fashion journalist must not only have an understanding of fashion, but also demonstrate a facility with words. As you read the provided descriptions, plan supplemental research relative to necessary skills. Fashion merchandising and marketing are both business-oriented fields with a creative side.

(below) Jingwen Xie, In the Dust of This Planet knits collection.

(above) Christian Dior exhibition 2019, V&A Museum, London.

As the fashion field rapidly adapts to issues such as the climate crisis, world health concerns, and political situations, the fields of public relations (PR) and trend forecasting could become increasingly important. Costume design is a hybrid field crossing entertainment and fashion. It is well suited as a direction for those with an interest in both fashion history and performance.

In the twentieth century, fashion design came to be recognized as an art, earning its place in museums and galleries. Fashion and textile conservation and archiving have grown with that acceptance. Established fashion houses, as well as independent designers, are developing increased understanding of the value of well-preserved archives in maintaining the history of their brand and collections.

Short- and long-term goals

Set both short- and long-term goals for your career. Early in a career, some designers with the ultimate goal of self-employment choose to start working under the tutelage of a well-established designer. Although rarely offering significant financial compensation, the knowledge gathered could build a substantial foundation for future self-employment.

The higher starting salaries and comprehensive benefits offered by corporations can become a decisive factor, depending on personal needs. Larger corporations are well suited to learning the marketing and development process. Here, each job is strongly focused: a designer will not work on technical areas of the website; a web designer will not be involved in garment creation. If you have already focused in on a personal direction, a job within a large corporate structure may be a good choice for you. Working with a single designer in a smaller organization offers the opportunity for broader exposure to many aspects of the business. More limited staffing requires everyone to pitch in to fill whatever needs arise. This could mean experience in everything from design to social media. This opportunity for a broad sampling of disciplines facilitates increased discovery.

(above) Yves Saint Laurent Museum, Paris.

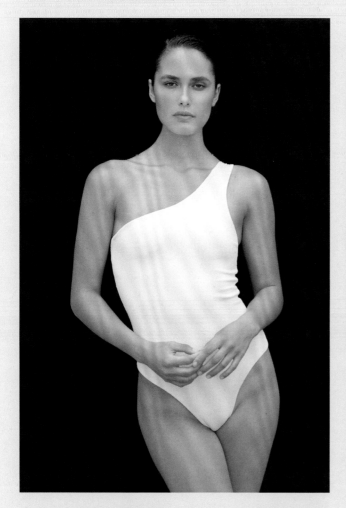

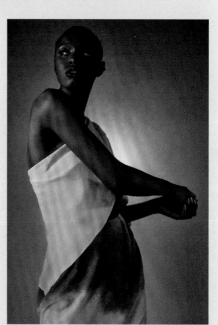

Fashion career paths

Fashion design

A designer often specializes in specific garment categories. In the extensive womenswear category these have traditionally included: sportswear or casual wear; formal daytime business wear; active sportswear; outerwear; intimate apparel—underwear, loungewear and sleepwear; and formal eveningwear for special occasions. Specialized areas also exist within menswear and childrenswear. Designers working in menswear may cover a broader range, designing casual sportswear as well as formal daytime and evening wear. A childrenswear designer will create casual and formal wear for both boys and girls. They all focus on creativity and style in form and function. In this competitive field, organization and the ability to work under pressure are requisites.

(opposite, clockwise from top left) Sara Cristina Villasmil, Beachwear/Leisurewear, Resort look-book, Summer 2020; casual menswear; Louise Hidinger, Sustainable Design: Zero Waste capsule collection; Ikshit Pande, QUOD menswear 2021 collection; Ian C. Gonzales, Audrey in Black evening dress, made of repurposed men's suits, an homage to Hubert de Givenchy.

(above) Diverse body types and sizes, intimate apparel.

Fashion technical design

This precision field requires a strong understanding of garment construction. It demands the analog or digital drawing skills necessary to represent garment details and construction lines in flat form.

(below) Technical drawings by Belinda Jacobs of Techpacks.co; precise digital blueprints of construction details in flat form.

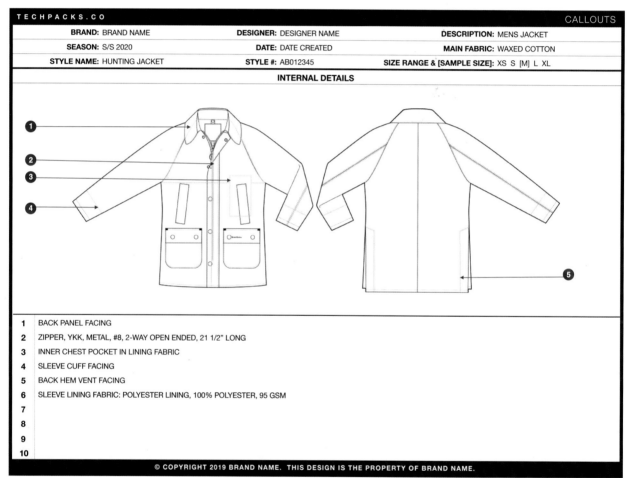

TECHPACKS.CO — CALLOUTS

BRAND: BRAND NAME	**DESIGNER:** DESIGNER NAME	**DESCRIPTION:** MENS JACKET
SEASON: S/S 2020	**DATE:** DATE CREATED	**MAIN FABRIC:** WAXED COTTON
STYLE NAME: HUNTING JACKET	**STYLE #:** AB012345	**SIZE RANGE & [SAMPLE SIZE]:** XS S [M] L XL

INTERNAL DETAILS

1	BACK PANEL FACING
2	ZIPPER, YKK, METAL, #8, 2-WAY OPEN ENDED, 21 1/2" LONG
3	INNER CHEST POCKET IN LINING FABRIC
4	SLEEVE CUFF FACING
5	BACK HEM VENT FACING
6	SLEEVE LINING FABRIC: POLYESTER LINING, 100% POLYESTER, 95 GSM
7	
8	
9	
10	

© COPYRIGHT 2019 BRAND NAME. THIS DESIGN IS THE PROPERTY OF BRAND NAME.

WHILE EVERY CARE IS TAKEN IN PRODUCING THIS JOB, TECHPACKS.CO MAKES NO WARRANTIES, EXPRESSED OR IMPLIED, OF MERCHANTABILITY, FITNESS FOR PURPOSE, OR OTHERWISE. IN THE EVENT OF ANY DISCREPANCY OR ERROR, THE LIABILITY OF TECHPACKS.CO IS THEREFORE LIMITED SOLELY TO THE REMUNERATION PAID TO TECHPACKS.CO BY THE CLIENT. IN NO EVENT SHALL TECHPACKS.CO HAVE ANY RESPONSIBILITY OR LIABILITY FOR DIRECT, INDIRECT, INCIDENTAL OR CONSEQUENTIAL DAMAGES INCURRED AS A RESULT OF ANY ERROR.

PAGE 4 OF 10

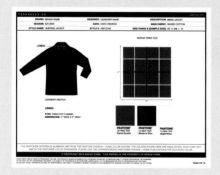

Patternmaking

This is a profession for the detail oriented with an understanding and love of garment construction. Proficiency in geometry and math are important components in pattern drafting. Knowledge of dedicated software is a plus.

(below, clockwise from left) Hands-on traditional pattern marking; user-friendly software by Lectra/Kaledo for digital pattern marking—computer-generated marking for efficient use of fabric; hands-on pattern marking assessment for efficient use of fabric.

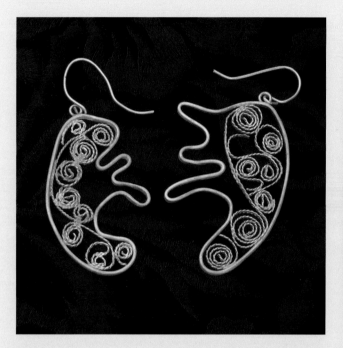

Production management

Overseeing the product development process, this position requires excellent organization, computer, and people skills. Integration of new software and emerging technologies can lower production costs, creating competitive advantage. This position maintains and improves efficiency and quality within the supply chain.

Accessories design

This category covers the design of all non-clothing fashion items. These include: gloves, belts, and handbags in natural and synthetic materials; footwear (shoes, hosiery); headwear (scarves, hats); and jewelry. An accessories designer requires category-specific skills. Some skills can be acquired in school; for example, relative to jewelry, digital 3D-design skills in SolidWorks or Rhinoceros are helpful for design and mass production. Learning sourcing and metal assembly may be closer to an apprenticeship process.

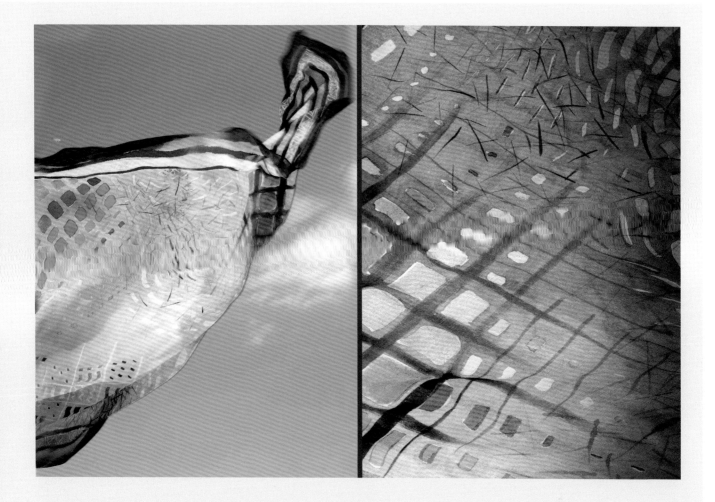

(opposite, left) Michelle Nahum-Albright, The Conversation, handmade silver filigree earrings.

(opposite, right) Michelle Nahum-Albright, Protect Me, handmade silver filigree necklace.

(above) Hand-painted silk scarf, Tamara Albu.

Textile design

This work requires a love of surface design married to an appreciation of material feel and texture. A strong understanding of woven and knitted material is also necessary. This should be supported by highly developed analog drawing and painting skills as well as digital-rendering skills.

100 years of
Fashion
Illustration

Cally Blackman

(above) *100 Years of Fashion Illustration* book cover with David Downton illustration and Marion Deuchars lettering.

Bespok[...]
v[...]

Fashion illustration

The illustrator represents the design of fashion goods in sketch form. This is generally freelance work and entails an understanding of fabric and an ability to capture the emotional as well as structural attributes of a garment. Depending on the illustrator's style, various techniques and media can be used: pencil, ink, watercolor, gouache, pastels, collage, mixed media or digital. Here, an understanding of the human form meets drawing and painting skills.

Retail management

In the broadest sense, this job is about the integration of customer relationship and brand management with sales. This is a "people" job, requiring knowledge of the fashion retail segment, strong communication skills, and the ability to understand and control the retail environment.

Fashion merchandising

A merchandiser has a combination of sharp aesthetic skills and an analytical mind. While this position supervises the creation of window, in-store and other visual displays, it also analyzes market trends, sales, production costs, and business projection direction.

Fashion buyer

A fashion buyer selects product for acquisition and distribution by their retailers. Working closely with designers and suppliers, the buyer makes product selections based on customer buying patterns and company budget. A variety of styles, sizes, and colors may be chosen to align with specific customer demographics, geographic locations, and overall assortment. Working with financial data provided by merchandisers, they make buying decisions as they assess trends in lifestyle, fashion details, styling, color, and fabrication.

(above) Selfridges, Oxford Street, London, decorated for Christmas and New 2020 Year.

Fashion marketing

A marketer positions and promotes brand and product, building consumer perception with the creation of strategy, visual positioning, and selection of promotional media. This work requires analysis and a critical mind. Media/trend research, advertising development, and in-store promotion, as well as pricing and distribution are all part of this job.

Public relations

This is a communications position, creatively sharing the story and experience of a brand with the public. A public relations professional nurtures relationships with fashion editors and stores as well as the target demographic. Visual, verbal, and written skills as well as strong problem-solving skills are required.

Fashion journalism

A fashion journalist reveals the story of the changing world of fashion. This primarily freelance job requires strong writing skills, curiosity, a love of fashion and trends, research ability, and digital proficiency. A journalism or writing degree is a plus, but not a must.

Fashion photography

A fashion photographer uses a camera to sell attitude and product. They bring fashion stories to life. Still lifes, environments, and models can work together or become the single focus of an image. Training may be acquired formally or informally, as long as the final photographic image tells the story visually. Images may be used in advertising or editorial for both print and digital media.

DJIUN

SENIOR DESIGNER
VMAGAZINE & VMAN — LAYOUT DESIGN

DJIUN

The 2019 Sunglass Hut campaign was inspired by the classic phrase "la vie en rose." Each unique pair of sunglasses that Gigi Hadid tries on magically shapes her perspective to experience a fun and exciting world within the store.

SENIOR DESIGNER
SUNGLASS HUT — 2019 VIDEO CAMPAIGN

(opposite) Elena Moussa, garment and headpiece.
(above) Djiun Wang, editorial fashion photography portfolio.

Fashion modeling

There are three primary types of model: runway, fitting, and editorial. The runway model promotes fashion collections through live shows. The fitting model is used in the garment development process to create the right relationship of garment to body size and shape; this model must meet the industry standard measurements for the average size (a US female model is size 8, for the UK the standard is size 10, and the EU uses size 38). A fitting model must maintain a constant body weight, be very patient, and able to stand still for long periods of time. Both male and female models work closely with the design team, providing feedback on garment wearability. The editorial model is featured in publication layouts and may present clothing in advertising or as an overall brand representative.

While size is important to all modeling functions, overall visual appearance and carriage are most valuable for runway and editorial models, who present brand attitude to the public. Most models are placed by specialized agencies such as Elite Model Management or Ford Models in the US. In Britain, the British Fashion Model Agents Association registers model agencies and independent agents and they are affiliated with the British Fashion Council. Vision Models, Nevs Models, and Hughes Models (of IMM Agency Group) are all reputable UK agencies.

(opposite) Runway show, It's Ethical Fashion, AltaRoma AltaModa July 2013.
(above) Mu-Tien Liu, portrait of artist Marz23.
(above, right) Alicia Mennen, designer/model portrait.
(right) Céline Haddad, Collection 1 hair and makeup styling.

Fashion styling

With a good eye for detail and trends, the stylist makes a designer or editorial vision come alive, bringing together all the right elements needed to make a statement. This includes shoes, hats, jewelry, and clothing. A stylist might work at photographic shoots for magazines and advertising, or be involved in creating the visual impact of live shows and videos. This is primarily a freelance field.

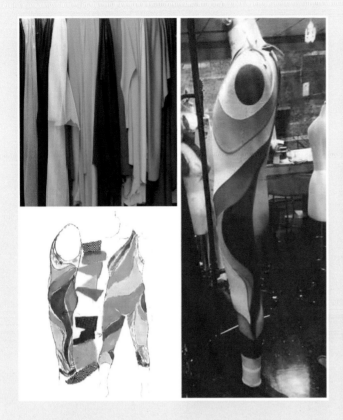

(above) Katrin Schnabl, costume design. "Beyond the Shore" design process and Aerosol scene.

(right) Katrin Schnabl, costume design. "Beyond the Shore", Aerosol scene performed by Rory Hohenstein and Christine Rocas.

Fashion/image consulting

This consultant is booked by companies or private clients needing assistance in defining their public image. Focusing on the effect of personal appearance on professional image, consulting takes into account hairstyle, makeup, body shape, personal preferences, and professional needs to create an enhanced perception of an individual in public settings. It is a derivative of fashion styling that can be recommended by public relations professionals.

Costume design

The costume designer creates for movement in live and filmed performances. This can include: dance, opera, drama, and music. With imagination, a solid knowledge of fashion history, and technical garment construction skills, they create to carry a story from script to character.

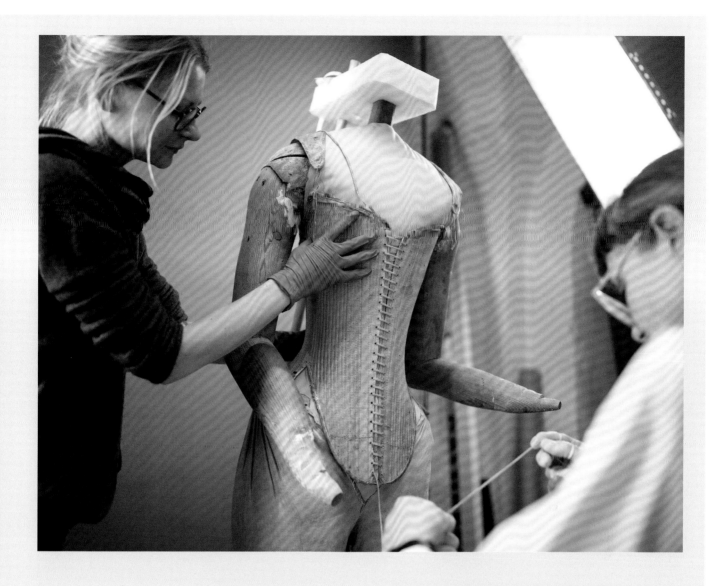

Fashion and textile conservation and archiving

A conservator must have a wide knowledge of textile history, costume history, and art history. Demanding patience, concentration, and meticulous labor, this line of work includes hands-on sewing skills as well as technical expertise in textile and garment construction. A background in organic chemistry aids in delicate restoration and preservation. Giving a second life to historical pieces which might otherwise perish forever is worth the tedious labor. Restoring textiles, garments, or accessories must come from deep love and passion for fashion history.

(above) Queen Elizabeth I's funeral corset being prepared to go on show at New Abbey Museum.

Fashion recruiting

Successful recruiters specialize and have strong communication skills. A fashion recruiter needs persistence, a good understanding of the industry's stratification, knowledge of the latest fashion trends, and great networking skills in order to locate and suggest just the right candidate to a client.

coloro + WGSN

Trend analyst

An analyst has an understanding of demographics, customer profile, product, and market trends. They investigate and analyze lifestyle, material, and color to predict applications for a variety of industries including fashion, beauty, home, and automotive.

(above) Luscious Red, Verdigris, Digital Lavender, Sundial and Tranquil Blue colour forecast for S/S 23 by WGSN, the leading global consumer trend forecaster, in partnership with Coloro, the color intelligence authority.

The Search

Navigating the search process can be complex. You know what you want. Your dedication and focus have created a cohesive personal brand strategy. To land the right job you will require an arsenal of tools, organized research, and effective planning.

You will be able to search more efficiently with the aid of a wish list, or target list, of companies, institutions, and organizations that interest you. This will help you to organize and prioritize your search. Often companies have a recruiting webpage on their website. Browsing posted openings for companies of interest is a great way to begin getting a sense of what positions are currently available.

Contacts

Begin reaching out to your network whenever you are ready to seriously begin a job search. If you already have a job and are considering a move, discreetly let your trusted network know. Talk to contacts who are connected to companies on your wish list. A personal recommendation is often the most direct way to gain access to hiring managers. Consider your network of relatives, friends, friends of relatives, former school colleagues, and professors. A professor who is open to giving advice and who believes in your qualifications and talent may even put you in touch with their own contacts.

Always be prepared to talk about your job search and show samples of your latest collection. Have a well-prepared PDF available for immediate use. This is a great use of your tablet or mobile phone. Whether dealing with a personal contact or someone entirely new, gauge each approach thoughtfully.

Recruitment agencies

There are specialized temporary employment agencies supplying freelance fashion and design talent to established companies. 24 Seven Talent and Creative Circle are well known in the US. In Canada companies know Style Nine to Five. Christian Bassett is an important name for recruiters in Europe and Asia. For young fashion professionals, contract work such as this can be a good beginning. It offers an inside look at a variety of firms. Decision-makers have a chance to discover your talents and evaluate your potential without concern about long term commitment. As a freelancer you can assess the pros and cons of working for that particular company. Making contacts and learning first-hand about the company values, internal policies, and structure is priceless. Not everyone is suited to the freelance lifestyle, so gauge your preference and needs carefully. A freelance assignment at a company on their wish list could be beneficial to those who are comfortable freelancing. If preferred companies on your wish list don't have immediate openings, widen your search to firms offering comparable opportunities in the desired field or specialization.

Headhunters

With a few years of industry experience under your belt, you may be contacted by "headhunters". These elite recruiting firms are regularly retained by clients to spot interesting talent. Headhunters do not place at a beginner level, these well-paid professionals usually work with significant middle to executive-level positions. Among the most renowned are French agency Floriane de Saint-Pierre et Associés and American agency Karen Harvey Consulting Group. Both of these specialize in placement for luxury and high end fashion. In Asia, the Indian fashion consultant Sabina Chopra and "the Oprah of China," Hung Huang, are among the most significant high-end recruiters. Lulu Kennedy, the British "fairy godmother of emerging London fashion," helms Fashion East, a British non-profit initiative which discovers young fashion designers and helps them become recognized for their exceptional talent.

Résumé and cover letter

Send out résumés in a measured, thoughtful manner. Address résumés and appropriate cover letters only to contacts provided by your network, carefully researched employers, or in response to advertised posts. A blanket mailing of your résumé is never a good idea. Your résumé and cover letter each play a crucial role in the job search process. Make sure both of them reflect your personal branding (see p.124–126) and customize both for every job application as discussed in Chapter 4.

References

You must be ready to provide references. Keep a list of names and contact information of those who have already granted permission to be contacted. These might be former employers or professors. It is always wise to keep these contacts informed about the possibility of an upcoming call.

(above) Emily Waters, sportswear porfolio plates.

Preparing for the Interview

Success! Your job application made the cut. Your cover letter and résumé were noticed and consequently you have been asked to interview. Before the interview, learn all you can about the company. Review collections and editorial photoshoots. Watch fashion show videos. Try to be familiar with collections going back several seasons. Read the reviews. Visit the company's social media pages.

Part of your homework is gathering as much information as possible about that firm, including the pay structure for the desired position. Websites such as Glassdoor or Indeed are useful for this research. They are constantly surveying and updating their database, providing company reviews, employees' testimonials, and salaries for various positions in each of their listed companies.

Adapting your portfolio

As you establish the short- and long-term goals for your career, make sure they are synchronized with the market targeted in your portfolio.

It is smart to begin with a master portfolio. The general content is created, organized, and curated to reflect immediate goals within your targeted field. Be aware that positions listed with the same title could well have different job description specifics for different companies. This is a key reason why your portfolio should be edited and updated for every single job interview. Maintain flexibility and objectivity, but never disregard the strategy or portfolio consistency that supports your signature style.

As an example, let's assume that you have a portfolio focusing on women's casual sportswear built to target a younger age group at a bridge price point. You spot an opening for a designer of this description, but it is in a mass-market sportswear company. There is still an opportunity here. Do your homework. The best chance for success comes from analyzing the company then selecting the appropriate design changes in order to customize your portfolio. For this market it might mean removing some extreme styles, or garments that are more labor intensive to manufacture.

Continual portfolio updating also provides an opportunity to represent yourself as a designer in tune with current trends, technologies, and industry events. Since artists and designers are usually the first to experiment with the latest technologies, consider featuring these innovations in your portfolio. Take advantage of any new discoveries or creations to freshen your portfolio on an ongoing basis.

The factsheet

Before your interview, create an informal factsheet. This is a listing of pertinent facts about the company to prepare you for the interview. Set them up in a format comfortable for you. A well-researched factsheet will describe the company characteristics and mission, guiding you in a portfolio editing assessment, and preparing you for interview discussions. Familiarizing yourself with the brand's latest collections and business news is part of this process. The company might have announced the opening of an overseas production facility, or the latest PLM software system implementation. Prompted by this, you could choose to add more technical sketches, tech packs, or digital designs to your existing or targeted marketing material. A current knowledge of the company may lead to beneficial interview discussion.

Interview attire

"What to wear?" Although at first this might seem frivolous, in the field of fashion it is an issue to be carefully addressed. To feel most at ease, select garments that present well and make you feel physically and emotionally comfortable. You are a representative of your personal brand image. The outfit must reflect your designer personality as well as fit in with the company image. Use your research as a guide to appropriate personal presentation. If interviewing for Calvin Klein you might choose a dusty, muted color palette with a minimalist cut rather than a bright, colorful outfit. An intricately patterned, detailed look in vivid tones would be more suitable for a Betsey Johnson interview.

Rehearsing

Whether you are invited to an in-person or a video interview, it is a good idea to rehearse your presentation. Prepare to give a very brief statement about your studies and prior work experience. You will have already made sure you are thoroughly familiar with the company you are interviewing with. Be able to describe briefly their targeted market, price point, and customer profile, giving a couple of examples of consumer shopping habits and competitive labels. You should be ready to highlight the essentials of your collections, pointing out the key details and unique elements of select styles in preparation for reviewing your portfolio with the interviewer. Make sure specific visual backgrounds, mood boards, and fabric boards introduce each separate concept. Expect to discuss the design element similarities of an entire group of garments belonging to the same unit theme rather than a single outfit. Be clear and concise—repeating yourself will reduce your allocated time. For example, if a collection of 15 looks is based on an A-line silhouette, it is sufficient to mention that fact once. Move on to describing the fabric story and the color palette, pointing out their use in a few particular designs.

Rehearse until you can fit the presentation into a maximum of ten minutes. It is helpful to video record your presentation. This will assist you in spotting verbal errors and any gestures or body language you might want to adjust. Look for overused words or phrases or uncomfortable body language such as fidgeting or clenching your hands.

The Interview

Depending on the size of the company, the first interview might be conducted by the human resources office (HR) over the phone or face-to-face. HR staff are always looking for general attributes that would be compatible with the company overview. Do your best to present well at all times. They have the role of screening candidates to make sure only those who are the best fit move on to the next step. These are screening professionals with a sharp ability to search for professional personality attributes. It would not be unusual to find yourself being tested indirectly. For example, a screener might try to gauge your ability to work in a pressured environment with tight deadlines by putting you on the spot during the interview. Being aware of possible HR tactics could help you modify your reactions, allowing you to move to the next step, which would be the face-to-face interview. For large or small companies, this interview is usually with one or more people from the team you are hoping to join, including the head designer. Make sure you are giving a polished impression, appropriate to the company culture. Finally, be sure to show your genuine interest.

If interview scheduling choices are being offered (regarding a face-to-face interview), it may be wise to select the most distant date. Any additional time available will give you more time to prepare.

In-person interview

Interviewing for a job can be a bit stressful, especially if you haven't done it before. Make sure you arrive for the interview about 15 minutes in advance. You'll be able to gather your thoughts and get ready mentally. For any interview have your résumé with you. Treat everyone you encounter respectfully.

You will probably meet the department's head designer and one or more members from the team you might join. Wait until you are offered a seat. The standard time for an interview in the US is about 15–20 minutes; make the best of the allocated time. You want to offer maximum information about your skills, talents, and potential. At the start of the interview you may be asked to say a few words about yourself, your studies, and previous work experience before moving on to showing your portfolio. Think of your portfolio as the beginning of a dialog between the interviewer and yourself. The head designer will be looking to see if your aesthetic sense and design skills are compatible with the company's image. They will also be evaluating whether you are a good fit for the design team and if there is a good "chemistry" between the two of you.

During the interview use your judgment, be flexible, and listen to your instincts. Sometimes the interviewing designer will leaf through your portfolio. Other times you will lead them through it. You always want to hold audience interest, so if you detect the slightest sign of boredom or impatience in your interviewer, adjust the pace or skip some portions of your presentation.

(opposite, top left) Sebastian Tjsie showcases his strong drawing skills on a promotional card clearly coordinated with his business card.

(opposite, top right) Chang Shao creates compact promotional cards illustrating a range of skills, from mood board through design and finished garment.

(opposite, below) Your attire should be in line with the culture of the interviewing company. Consider whether this is casual or more formal.

(right) Tamara Albu's digital portfolio being shown on a tablet. When interviewing, be prepared to show your portfolio on portable devices.

For you, the interview's main objective is to be hired, but it also presents an opportunity for both parties to learn about each other. If you are invited to ask questions you'll have a chance to gather useful information first-hand. Be prepared with a set of questions that indicate interest in the firm's operation and market for use as needed.

The conversation can move in unexpected directions. Go with it.

If the time permits, the interviewing designer will usually be glad to answer your questions, show some of their latest designs, and talk about the department. Reserve salary and benefits inquiries for later discussions, during the follow-up interviews.

Remote interview

Over the last few years the popularity of remote interviews has grown. Safety precautions related to the Covid-19 global pandemic made this process a necessity in almost all instances.

Familiarity with GoToMeeting, Teams, Zoom, and other teleconferencing applications has become a job search essential. A face-to-face interview with a potential employer from a different city or country could have once required traveling and accommodation expenses. Use of the video conferencing platforms can both extend possibilities and eliminate this expense. The remote interview format allows the participation of multiple stakeholders, regardless of their location. An interview could easily be recorded to be reviewed with associates unable to attend.

While an interview via teleconference requires the same preparation as for an in-person interview, there are a few other things to remember. This type of communication necessitates a secure, comfortable, neat, and quiet place to speak from. On-screen, it is just as important to pay attention to your grooming and making sure your attire reflects the standards of the hiring company. Be aware of how the camera sees you and maintain a professional demeanor. Just as you would with an in-person interview, have your cover letter and résumé handy in case you need to refer to them. In all interviews keep your answers brief and to the point.

Follow-up interviews

Being asked to return for a follow-up interview is a good indication that the interview went well. You made the shortlist of preferred candidates. A second interview is usually set up with additional decision-makers. The meeting may be held as a group conference or be a string of one-to-one interviews. Be prepared to do an abbreviated form of your presentation, leaving room for discussion of the details of the position you are applying for. Check normal regional procedure for reviewing the working hours or annual compensation: this may include salary, overtime policy, bonuses, health insurance, vacation time, advancement opportunities, and training.

Whenever possible let the interviewer reveal specific numbers. If you are pressed to give a salary number, it would be wise to offer a range. When salary and benefits are revealed, take your time to think them over. "Let me think about it," or "When will you expect my answer?" are common replies.

During the course of your presentation or interview, make sure you interact with everyone attending the meeting. This is key. If asked a question, avoid directing your answer only to the person asking the question. By making eye contact with all meeting participants you will be able to inspire confidence and project stability. This approach provides the additional benefit of being able to assess the audience interest and make changes to presentation pace as necessary.

The investor's interview

For designers looking to start their own business, an investor interview can be pivotal. Obtaining outside financing support is not an easy task. Once you have found a potential investor willing to meet with you, be prepared with the research and planning necessary to convince them of the validity of your concept. Have a clear understanding of the investor's expectations. Develop a solid and well-researched business plan defining the nature of your business, its goals, and a schedule of stages to achieve those goals.

The promotional interview

This type of interview is conducted by potential retail buyers. The interviewer may be either the designer of an independent label, a PR representative, or one of the regional sales associates of a larger corporation. This kind of meeting aims to help you promote new collections, establish future business terms, and/or establish new or continuing collaborations. The buyer's goal is to get acquainted with your styles while making suggestions based on their organization's projected merchandise numbers. Depending on the business commitment, buyers might make requests for additional adjustments to collections, such as requesting popular colorways or the addition of past best-selling pieces.

(above) Lou Malta, series of cards to promote her designs across multiple disciplines.

Following up—emails, calls, or cards

Once you have interviewed, there may be an unnerving silence as the employer continues their round of interviews and deliberates. Sometimes there are changes within the company that create delays. Don't just wait, follow up. Do your best to keep the momentum going. Consider three levels of follow-up. Immediately after the interview send a handwritten note or at least a short email. If you haven't heard in a week or so, send a second email. In a few weeks, call or send another follow-up note in writing or by email. If you have heard any news about the company, adding a comment reinforces your continued interest.

When worded properly, these polite, respectful communications remind the interviewer of your special skills as well as your enthusiasm. If you neglected to mention any important information during the interview, include it here. As a creative you have the advantage of being able to include a PDF with a few new or particularly interesting samples of your work. Make sure the graphics in this PDF match your personal identity system. Never send anything without clear contact information.

Review

The interview is part of a larger process. Before you reach that stage, you will set both short- and long-term goals and develop a personal brand strategy. This will be reflected in your targeted search and all of your social media, portfolio, and printed materials. Your résumé, cover letter, and business card will clearly represent you to potential employers.

Research all the fashion-affiliated fields that interest you to focus in on specific categories where your skills might fit well. You are looking for a match that will let you grow.

Your broad research will include: developing a network and locating all available employment resources; visiting innovative retailers; and being aware of new developments in the industry .

Dos and Don'ts

Do take time to research the variety of careers the fashion industry and related fields can offer

Don't limit the fashion career paths you consider solely to the designing of garments

Do extensively research any company you are interested in, including collections, reviews, and new business developments

Don't forget to tailor both your résumé and portfolio to highlight work and attributes most attractive to your interviewer

Do have a flexible plan as to how you will describe yourself and your work during your 15–20 minutes with an interviewer

Don't forget to personally present yourself in a manner aligned with the company's visual and conceptual values

Do remember to follow up after an interview with a polite email or handwritten note

Don't make a nuisance of yourself—time your follow-ups appropriately

Quick Quiz

· Why should you rehearse for an interview?

· Who will normally be present during your first interview for a large company?

· How many interviews can you expect?

· What are the two main things a head designer will be looking for in a candidate?

· During which phase of the interview process would you discuss salary and other compensation?

(opposite) Dover Street Market at Dover Street, London. Cubes attached to floor, wall and ceiling, being used as shelving. Architect: Rei Kawakubo, 2006.

Designer Profiles

Céline Haddad
Céline Haddad Studio

Agatha Agatha
Raccoonandbabies

Hannah Dean
Burberry

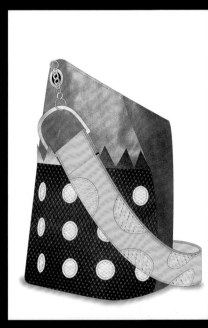

Ikshit Pande
QUOD

Qing Guo
Beijing Institute of
Fashion Technology

Olga Singh
Bun Collection
0.5 Redesign

CÉLINE HADDAD

Céline Haddad Studio,
Founder and Artistic Director
Beirut, Lebanon and Paris, France

Céline Haddad is a French–Lebanese designer. Influenced by her life in Beirut, London, Paris, and New York, balancing elegance and edge she creates garments for a global urban customer. With a sensuality, independence, and power, soft meets hard in provocative, surprising forms. This is evidenced by her first solo showcase at the 2019 Vancouver Fashion Week.

Where did your passion for fashion originate?
I have always been intrigued by the fashion industry but never thought I'd be a part of it. Before studying fashion design at Parsons, New York, I completed a bachelor's in business administration (BBA) at the American University of Beirut. I felt my business degree was not challenging enough, and in checking online classes I stumbled upon a certificate in the management of luxury fashion companies. I decided to explore the fashion world further through courses, certificates, and internships. By the time I completed my BBA I had tackled fields including fashion journalism creative direction, management and marketing of luxury brands, blogging business, and fashion design. I fell in love with every area of the fashion industry, but I opted for design.

What was the most difficult part of your transition from student to fashion professional?
When you are in school you have set deadlines, clear projects, and professors to supervise you. When you are your own boss you are free, but need to be self-disciplined. Success is not for the faint of heart.

I'm not saying it's impossible to succeed early on, but it requires transitioning from being a dreamer to becoming a doer. Decision-making has to come fast and easy. Time has to be well planned and organized, and budget has to be well thought out and strict. Dealing with suppliers, orders, manufacturers, buyers, stylists, customers, and media can be quite overwhelming. To provide a taste of the reality of the field, I would highly recommend doing internships while still a student.

What drives you to move forward?
Challenge and wanting to do good move me forward, even during tough days. Being a fashion entrepreneur, I get to do different tasks every day. This makes it fun and creates diversity.

I'm hoping to contribute to improving the fashion industry by designing long-lasting garments. Made of high-quality materials, they are intended to outlast short-term trends. Having a story behind every garment and accessory makes it unique and special. Every single one of my creations has a meaning and is part of a bigger story. I hope this makes people talk about these topics.

What do you view as the most important qualities for an emerging designer?
Ambition, audacity, creativity, commitment, determination, self-discipline, organization, patience, perseverance, and passion.

What do you wish you knew when beginning your business?
I wish I had taken it more seriously when people warned me it would become my obsession. Although I've learned to plan my time well, my business is always on my mind. I live and breathe for my brand. I am responsible for its existence, wellbeing, and development. Since my brand is eponymous, it means that I am the face of my business, so my actions might affect it, and vice-versa. A professional mistake or failure might impact me directly as a person—we have a shared reputation and name.

How does fashion design fit into a radically changing world?
Fashion will always fit into a radically changing world. Since ancient Egypt fashion has influenced and has been influenced by our life and culture. Today, fashion

(above) Céline Haddad, look-book pages, Collection 1.

(above) Céline Haddad, runway, Collection 1.

design is a global economic sector that generates billions and creates job opportunities worldwide. It can even be viewed as a network of industries, because it encompasses activities from production of raw materials and manufacturing of finished garments to their distribution and sale. But fashion design does not limit itself to the creation of *things*, it is about creating lifestyle and dreams. Fashion can be misinterpreted as a minor subject not meriting attention, but fashion has a strong role in society and modern culture. With the rise of social media, fashion has become a major topic of discussion with the potential to create change while adapting quickly to the changes around it. The consumer decides what is fashionable, but fashion designers use their industry as a means of communication and change. Designers raise awareness on important topics such as human rights, sustainability, and animal welfare.

How would you like a customer to feel when they wear your clothes?

One of my main goals is to empower women. Confidence comes with feeling comfortable in what you are wearing. It is very important to me that my customer feels worthy, confident that she can achieve her goals, while confident in her body and femininity.

I would also like my customer to feel liberated, playful, and free to express her individuality by adapting my creations to her own personal style. I revisit wardrobe classics and add a subtle modern touch to them, making sure they remain versatile in order to fit any body in an effortlessly stylish manner. Because my label is sustainable, I want my customer to feel guilt free, proud of owning my creations. In every garment there is an important meaning.

AGATHA AGATHA

RACCOONANDBABIES,
Founder and Creative Director
Jakarta, Indonesia

The designer behind the jewelry brand Raccoonandbabies, Agatha Agatha (CFDA+ nominee), integrates childhood memories from her upbringing in Indonesia with her worldly experiences studying design in New York City. Her jewelry has been featured in *Grazia, Nylon, Elle, Cosmopolitan, Femina,* and *Monaco* magazines as well as *The Jakarta Post.* www.raccoonandbabies.com

What initially drew you to the competitive field of jewelry design?
I've always been interested in toys and 3D objects so when I studied at Parsons School of Design it really showed me that I was more into jewelry than clothing. Fortunately, I was able to take 3D-modeling classes while I was completing my Fashion Design major, and after graduating from Parsons I went to the Fashion Institute of Technology to study jewelry. I then worked as a jewelry designer in Palm Beach for a while before I moved back to Jakarta and pursued Raccoonandbabies full time.

Who is the Raccoonandbabies customer?
Customers of RACCOONANDBABIES are both males and females who appreciate timeless and playfully sophisticated jewelry with refined, subtle details. We are mostly known for our collectible pieces with very distinctive designs. Most jewelry designs out there are very precious but for me, jewelry should be fun. I get inspired by toys and memories from my childhood and these collections have become the signature

pieces of RACCOONANDBABIES, especially the Arm Me collection.

Where does your inspiration for a new collection come from?

When I design, I always think about what kind of jewelry I'd like to wear and I start from there to create the shape. Sometimes I get inspired by seeing random objects and start making a collection from there. Like the VALUE.ABLE collection, which was inspired by zero waste jewelry that mimics the shapes of normally disposable plastic items.

What was most difficult about founding your own business?
Developing and maintaining self-discipline as an entrepreneur. It can be difficult to delineate between work and leisure time; having a definite start and finish time is often hard when you love what you do.

What advice would you give to a young designer aiming to develop their own brand?
Jewelry is very personal. It should offer an eye-catching recognizable designer style. I think it's important for designers to have strong brand identities, each appealing to the chosen markets. It is also very important to set the right price point for your brand; it dictates who your customers are, what kind of marketing tactics you will use, and the quality you will be able to produce in that range.

How would you reimagine the fashion industry as the world shifts to a new normal?
Valuable jewelry doesn't have to be boring; you can have fun and playful jewelry appropriate for any occasion. My jewelry is timeless, classic, distinctive, and individual. We always use the finest quality materials so that our pieces can be enjoyed for years to come.

What artist, writer, or designer inspires you?
Jean-Charles de Castelbajac! He created the teddy bear coat worn by Madonna and Helena Christensen. His work is heavily inspired by Pop Art color and wearable art. He is a fashion designer as well as an artist and it shows in his clothing.

(opposite) Agatha Agatha, Raccoonandbabies, promotional imagery.

HANNAH DEAN

Burberry, Product Development Assistant
London, UK

After graduating with a degree in Fashion Design, specializing in menswear, from the University of Leeds, Hannah moved to London to work in menswear design and development. As an undergraduate, her team won Burberry's "B Innovative Hackathon" competition. This focused on the redesign of Burberry's iconic trench coat; a pivotal moment in launching her current career, as Hannah now works for Burberry. Her creativity becomes clear in her eye for both detail and overview.

enlîst
A/W19

Describe your transition from student to young professional.

After the elation of graduating, I faced the challenge of breaking into a competitive industry. And I quickly realized that perseverance was as important as creativity and academic achievement.

I got "my break," starting my fashion career at Burberry as a supply chain assistant. It was a radically different role to anything I had envisioned. I worked to utilize excess raw materials to create a more sustainable supply chain. I later assumed my current role as a product development assistant for the seasonal ready-to-wear collections. So I have worked at the beginning and the end of Burberry's supply chain. Challenges have included post-Brexit manufacturing and global pandemic operations. I am continually learning.

Discuss your job search strategy upon leaving school.

Informed by my internship at Margaret Howell, I knew I wanted to work in high-end fashion but different facets of the business inspired me. This led me to focus my search on a market sector rather than a specific role. I applied for a variety of positions across design and production. Actively keeping my search broad enabled me to locate more opportunities. I gained a better understanding of what employers were looking for and honed my interview skills.

How have you built connections with other young and established fashion industry professionals?

It is inspiring to hear another person's career journey and I have gained useful career advice in relaxed, casual settings. Attending professional industry events or conferences has also been a great opportunity to connect with other fashion professionals and deepen my understanding of industry topics.

Internal welt chest pocket

Patch chest pocket
with additional pen/paintbrush
pockets

Covert welt pocket
below zip fastening

INSIDE VIEW

Sharing my recent workplace experiences with students at my alma mater has been an invaluable opportunity to get to know the next cohort of fashion professionals. I use social media to make myself available to those navigating their own job search journey. It has become a mutually rewarding experience.

Corporate-sponsored competitions can lead to further opportunities. Team success in the Burberry B Innovative Hackathon was rewarded with one-to-one mentoring sessions with Burberry department heads. This experience proved invaluable when I applied for my position at Burberry.

Which are the most important assets that made your job interview successful?
I was prepared to answer a wide variety of specific questions, and I presented myself as confident and genuine. I clearly demonstrated my values and beliefs. In this collaborative industry, it is imperative to work well with colleagues.

(opposite) Hannah Dean, Enlist collection A/W 2019: digital collage illustrations.

(above) Hannah Dean, Pentland Churchill Wardrobe Competition cover page: mixed media, hand-drawn and digital illustration.

Once hired, in what way did you need to adapt to the culture of your new employer?
I had to learn to "keep the pace". Mental agility and flexibility are key to success when working for a high-end brand. React quickly and problem solve continuously. Self-directed school assignments do not fully reflect the challenges of real-life collaborations. A calm and composed manner under pressure is a learned skill.

Striking the correct balance between creativity and commerciality, weighing factors such as cost, quality, aesthetics, and strategy is imperative. Adopting a commercial mindset means understanding the value of profit.

IKSHIT PANDE

QUOD, Founder and Artistic Director
New York, USA and New Delhi, India

At fashion label QUOD (short for the Latin *Quod erat demonstrandum* meaning "thus it has been demonstrated"), Ikshit Pande creates collections that fuse femininity, classic tailoring, and modern streetwear. In 2019 Ikshit showed at NYFW at the Pier and was one of the three winners of India's prestigious Blenders Pride Fashion Tour's mentorship program, The Platform. His work has been featured in magazines including *Vogue, GQ, ELLE, METAL, Interview, L'OFFICIEL, Numero, SICKY, Rolling Stone India*, and many more. www.quodnewyork.com

What is the mission and philosophy of QUOD?
The idea behind QUOD was to explore what it means to dress in the twenty-first century. I believe fashion designers are not given proper credit in the anthropological world. When one goes back in time to study a certain period and its people, what they wore speaks of who they actually were.

There is not one philosophy behind QUOD but a few key values. We strip down the excess, building upon the very minimum to accentuate what may be hidden but is still right before the eyes. It's about playing with the essence of things, finding new meanings in them.

In what ways did your studies prepare you for founding QUOD?
Parsons School of Design is where I learned the basics of fashion design and garment construction. A summer at Central Saint Martins further contributed to my design thinking, sharpening my vision. I had no plans whatsoever of starting my own brand right after school (in fact it was quite the opposite—I wanted to work for an established design house). But in one class we developed a personal brand concept. A lot of thinking for QUOD happened right there, including the name. All I had to do after school was refine my graduate collection for market and build upon the brand concept that was already in place.

For eight years before starting your own label you worked in advertising and brand management. Did this experience contribute in the development of QUOD?
One hundred percent.

I came into design with a very clear love of what I did in the past. And that's different. I met a lot of people who were choosing to change their career by going back to school, rather than extend their interests forward. I chose my particular course of study because it allowed me to apply my prior experience to my new field. It was very important for me to not give up being what I was but transform my experience into something more creatively rewarding.

My past as an advertising and brand management professional definitely helped me handle the business aspect of things better. It is a gift to be able to put on my business hat to decide what goes to the runway and how a concept may eventually be redone for the shelves.

Since starting your brand, what is the most important thing you have learned?
The most important learning is the value of the right timing. Clichéd but true; it is always for the best if things happen at the right time. With respect to fashion, it can mean the time you get your first repeat purchase, or the time when you win your first wholesale account. One has to be ready for the kind of success one dreams of or it can be fatal to a business.

What was the process of assembling the perfect team to bring your vision to reality?
I did not have a set process. My method was very organic. It really began with accepting and noting my own strengths and weaknesses, so that I could work with people who do certain things much better than I do. After years of working in typical hierarchical team structures I realized I prefer to work in a collective

format. By collective, I mean a bunch of individuals who do great work in their own areas yet contribute to a common vision without being driven by one supervisor who's at watch. The QUOD brand is seeded upon this notion as well—of a collective.

This was an important reason why I did not want to name the brand after one person, myself. I truly believe design is a collaborative endeavor.

How do you view the role of color in both garment collections and branding?

Even though QUOD is primarily perceived as a monochromatic brand, working in black and white, we choose to use color in our collections in very targeted ways.

When one closes one's eyes, a strong and consistent color stays for a few seconds until everything dissolves. I see more value in the memory of the color than its immediate effect.

Where do you find inspiration?

Men and women—how they dress and style themselves, people on the streets, nature in a huge way, architecture and shapes of objects, historical events and periods. There are a lot of things that inspire me, although I do keep going back to nature. Perhaps because of being born and brought up in the foothills of the Himalayas. Whatever the inspiration may be, a thorough study of it and experiments with humanization of that concept are key in developing any of my collections.

(left) Ikshit Pande, QUOD A/W 2021–22 collection.

QING GUO

Beijing Institute of Fashion Technology,
Assistant Professor of Fashion Accessories
Beijing, China

After graduating with an MFA in Accessory Design from the Savannah College of Art and Design and working as a designer for Fleabag, a New York luggage and accessories business, Qing Guo returned to Beijing to teach and pursue her fashion career. An ambitious young designer herself, Qing Guo guides her students at Beijing Institute of Fashion Technology toward independent, innovative fashion ideas. Her bold and graphic accessories vibrate with a colorful, playful, positive energy.

As a teaching assistant, she works in the accessories department on a variety of courses: footwear design, sewing tech, CAD, handbag patternmaking and structure, and portfolio development.

What drives your interest in accessories?
Accessories provide a flexible way for people to add excitement to their outfits. In the same manner as clothing, accessories express a designer's aesthetic and conceptual perspective. I am a pragmatic designer. While I love all of fashion, I chose accessories as a practical and expressive path with growing opportunities after graduation.

How do you see the field of accessories changing as the fashion industry evolves?
Chinese consumers are dedicating more attention to a coordinated look of clothing and accessories, which means that Chinese brands are strengthening or developing new accessories departments. This means overall development of the category and an increase in opportunities in the sector.

All over the world, people are changing their consumption habits. Fast fashion is rapidly declining as consumers seek better, more durable, and eco-friendly products. This new attitude affects sectors from garments to shoes.

What do you see as the most exciting fashion opportunities in the Chinese market?
Due to the rapid development of the Internet and 5G networks, China leads the world in e-commerce development. New sales models are thriving: these include social media KOL [Key Opinion Leader] marketing, short video clips, and "seckills" (the instant sell out of newly advertised merchandise). Consumers, especially Millennials and Generation Z, no longer blindly consume luxury brands. They crave expressions of uniqueness, making them willing to pay for interesting niche product from start-up brands. Continuing technological progress and ongoing development of the internet has created opportunity for the rapid start-up and marketing of these fledgling brands.

How does Chinese training differ from the Western model?
The design departments of Chinese schools heavily integrate the practical manufacturing aspects of fashion. Emphasis is placed on sourcing, merchandising, quality control, trade fairs, and even taking part in negotiations with buyers. In order to further understand the needs of their future workplaces, students have the opportunity to prototype their designs at factories. This is possible due to a huge, accessible pool of factories in China.

When I studied at Savanah School of Art and Design, portfolio development was core. The courses were focused on cultivating talent for the design departments within fashion companies. Students were required to complete an education in production and process on their own.

What are the biggest challenges a young designer faces in developing their own product line in China?

The biggest challenge currently is matching designers' aesthetic choices to realistic market desires. Funding, operation and maintenance, publicity, and distribution channels are also great challenges for any start-up brand.

In the past decade, there have been many start-ups developed by emerging designers who have returned from overseas training. They benefit from favorable business policies for returned students. Even though many of these start-up brands have created eye-catching designs, they fail to appeal to the market and disappear very quickly.

What artist, writer, or designer inspires you?

I admire Japanese artists and designers Yayoi Kusama and Rei Kawakubo. Japan has done a good job of merging the inherited values and aesthetics of traditional Eastern culture with modern innovation. These two artist/designers have developed unique designs incorporating stylistic elements typical of Japanese culture with forward-thinking Western ideas. I am inspired to learn from their global perspective and bring more Chinese cultural elements into my own modern designs.

(below) Qing Guo accessories designs, Happy Shark collection.

OLGA SINGH

0.5 Redesign, Founder and Artistic Director
New York, USA and Moscow, Russia

Brooklyn-based Olga Singh suggests you radically rethink your wardrobe, redesigning existing clothing into remarkable new creations. With 0.5 Redesign, the client and designer come together to create a custom garment and unique experience. Each contributes half. Based on a client-provided garment, Olga develops a unique design. 0.5 Redesign: your clothes (0.5) + redesign (0.5) = our result (1).
05redesign.com

What inspired 0.5 Redesign?

I was running my brand of knit clothing, the BUN Project, which was quickly expanding in Moscow and already selling in ten stores. But when I tried to get my items into New York's showrooms, rejections followed: the 50/50 wool-acrylic mix in my items wasn't sustainable. "Sus... what?" I would wonder, nonplussed. I'd been sure I was at the forefront of responsible production, helping knitting single moms earn money with their handmade creations. That, as I learned, was a good start, but the items in my collection were impossible to recycle. And that was that!

I decided to completely reimagine my project. My inspiration was NYC-living itself. Manhattan, with its constant events, exhibitions, and brunches, was full of successful, beautiful, health-conscious people and social events were all about the wow! factor. Once, when I knew I needed to shine but had nothing to wear, I pulled out a box with projects from

my Parsons days. Right on top I found an unfinished blazer with the lining and sleeves sewn on wrong. I took a pair of scissors to it and voilà, I had... a scarf! It was a hit! I started coming up with something new from old clothing for each event I went to. And that's when I got it—this was it, 100% sustainable fashion. Eventually, I started getting orders.

How do clients grow or change from working with 0.5 Redesign?

Clients change to the degree that they are interested in changing. Those who have no interest in sewing buy our finished upcycled clothes, or give us their own garments for us to redesign to their specifications. Those who want to come up with their own design and learn to sew can attend classes in person or online. It's incredible to watch clients' eyes light up; I see them get inspired to do redesign. People who attend my classes start to really value clothing. They learn the time it takes to alter garments and they get a sense of what clothes should cost.

Why does zero waste fashion matter?

Zero waste principles are now a culture and a way of life for me. Striving for zero waste matters not just in fashion, but also when it comes to family, time, money, and even our emotional states. To survive these difficult times, when nature itself seems to be turning against humanity, we shouldn't try to change nature or go around it. We need to change ourselves and our relationship with the environment.

Are there other ways to create fashion garments that are not wasteful?

Of course, I'm all for finding new technologies to recycle existing fabric and limiting production of cloth from new raw material. But this is more on the side of global fashion and big business. Since my own business is still small, I'm taking baby steps and focusing on upcycling. I would love to give people new ideas or provide redesign models for clothing on a B2C (business-to-consumer) basis. Another vision is a global network where people share pictures of their clothing and can then send it to others who want it or contribute ideas for redesign. We could have a community of like-minded people helping one another.

Olga Singh, BUN Knits collection. Photo: Olga Singh; model: Karina Erzunova.

Olga Singh, 0.5 Redesign project.

How do you see your concept fitting into the evolving new normal of fashion?

My concept is a perfect fit for the idea of fashion's new normal. We have both online and off-line classes. Online, we have groups of up to six people who meet on Zoom to redesign their clothes. We meet and sew our pieces in real time. One class focuses on one piece for each client. Sometimes we see what we have and start sewing, while on other occasions we discuss ideas for redesign, give each other feedback, and continue sharing ideas after the lesson.

What was the most interesting garment created by 0.5 Redesign?

The most interesting garments are those the student-clients create. I watch how people who haven't studied sewing drape their own clothes and how they finish the edges. These student-clients create the most extraordinary pieces, which they then wear with pride and tell others that they made themselves.

I had a young man attend my three-hour jacket workshop. He'd just graduated from tenth grade. Every year, his parents would buy him a navy suit for his school uniform. He showed me two suits and said he was ready to cut them up. Three hours later he couldn't believe what he'd been able to make. He'd unstitched the sleeves on one suit to make a vest, leaving the shoulders. On the other suit, he'd cut a third of the blazer vertically and stitched the edges with white thread. The best part was that he hadn't planned to ever wear these jackets again, but after the work he put in his creations were his new favorites.

Endmatter

Glossary: working definitions

Alternation method: used to describe the fluctuated sequence in which portfolio units are organized. Together, the alternation and progression methods are used for achieving the maximum portfolio impact.

Analog format: used to mean tactile, physical printed or non-screen-based media. This takes into account the material quality of an object.

Block layout: several elements that are similar are grouped together. These blocks are organized to achieve a well-balanced composition with an emphasis on a specific focal point. For instance, a spread layout may contain a block of rendered sketches, a block of flats, and a block of swatches. In most cases the emphasis is on the rendered sketches block, which will be the largest among this layout.

Blog: a shortened version of weblog. It is an interactive, regularly refreshed website or section of a website for sharing the opinions, commentary, or work of an individual or group.

Brand: the overall perception of a product or product grouping as unique. It creates a shared experience through a set of recognizable features that distinctly identify a seller's goods or service as separate from others. This can be manifested in a name, logo, color scheme, and type choice.

Buyer: a professional who evaluates fashion product and makes retailer purchase decisions for a retail company and the targeted customer the company is focused on. Buyers analyze, plan, and negotiate based on cost, trends, and customer demographics.

Channels–social media: participation-based, interactive digital technologies that facilitate shared information creation or exchange via connecting networks or communities with similar interests. They can be accessed immediately by desktop computers or mobile devices such as laptops, phones, and tablets.

Collection: a group of merchandise developed for the retail market with a unified point of view, offered within a selected time frame or season. For fashion, a grouping may consist of garments, accessories, or footwear.

Color palette: a group of colors featuring specific hues and tones used to unify or give meaning to a given pattern, group of fashion product, or a brand.

Colorways: a range of color groupings in which fashion product or a given pattern is available

Construction: the appropriate application of sewing techniques such as stitches, seams, darts, gathers, pleats, and edge finishing to build a finished garment. A pattern template outlines the parts of a garment to be traced onto fabric before being cut out and assembled.

Consumer: a person who consumes or utilizes goods or products to satisfy personal needs not directly related to business activities.

Croquis: derives from the French meaning "sketch". In fashion, it refers to a quick figure sketch showing off the garments being created.

Customer profile: a detailed description of your target customer, including their needs, desires, and lifestyle. Demographic, geographic, and psychographic characteristics are used as a guide in creating appropriate collections and retail assortments.

Demographic: defines a segment of the population or a target audience with selected characteristics.

Digital format: images or files meant to be viewed on a screen. This is the opposite of a physical or analog format.

Digital presence: the overall impression of an individual or a brand conveyed online. This can be built through posted social media content, proprietary websites, and tagging for search engine tracking.

Distribution: a commercial business-to-business process involving five fundamental stages: forecast, production, launch, sales, and delivery. The process runs from six weeks to several months depending on the retail distribution level.

Fabric story: a group of cohesive fabrics and trims, gathered and presented to support the development of a garment or accessories collection.

Fabrication: the process of creating and manufacturing a style in a selected fabric.

Flats: also known as technical sketches. These are detailed accurate representations of garments. They are developed to assist patternmakers and factory production. They detail design, construction seams, and stitching.

Follower: a user of a social media network who receives constant updates and chooses to see all of another user's posts. Getting followers is a key aim for online businesses.

Format: the way in which elements are arranged, including shape, size, and organization.

Gender fluid: related to individuals who do not identify themselves as having a fixed or specific gender.

Grid: a network of uniformly spaced perpendicularly intersecting horizontal and vertical lines used as guide for locating elements on a page or in a space.

Hashtags: used in social media, a keyword or phrase preceded by the symbol # to classify or categorize text on Twitter.

Headhunter: also known as a recruiter. A headhunter reaches out to candidates for high-level positions, often on a retainer basis. A recruiter works with the broader hiring process. In a corporate structure, they are often in-house staff.

Host—website: providing space on a web server to store website data. This is how a website (including code, images, etc.) becomes available for online viewing.

Identity: clear communication of a distinct concept or character, including the qualities, values, and beliefs that distinguish it.

Line-sheet: listing size and color range; provides information on fashion product for wholesale sales and inventory tracking.

Logo/Logotype: a simple, recognizable, abstract or figurative graphic mark used to repeatedly identify a brand or product. It may often be a typographic representation of a brand's name.

Look-book: helps a company reach out to potential clients by presenting a fashion collection with high-quality images and product descriptions in a stylized context.

Market segmentation: a division of a target market into approachable groups based on price, lifestyle, needs, and common interests.

Mood board: visually evocative physical or digital collages that position images, textures, and dimensional elements such as fabric to represent a collection's attitude and mood.

Personal brand: the consistent perception or public persona expressing values and expertise created by an individual as a combination of graphic elements and experience.

Pose: a figure attitude to present the garment on the human body in fashion sketching or photography.

Price point: refers to a potential profitable price category within a set of market retail prices.

Progression method: used to describe a portfolio story line structure. Here, each unit is assigned to the key elements of the narrative and organized in ascending order. For any climaxing story line, this may be transitions from pastels to brights, from lights to darks, or from day to night. Together, the alternation and progression methods are used to achieve the maximum portfolio impact.

Prototype: an initial product model from which following production material is developed. In fashion, the most commonly used term for a prototype is "sample".

Raster: a part of dot matrix data structure. It represents a rectangular grid of pixels that is a standard for digitally saved or viewed images. The file size measurement DPI (dots per inch) is the measurement of these rasters/pixels.

Rendering: figurative drawings of fashion designs shown in a stylized manner. Rendered sketches accurately depict silhouette and details in addition to suggesting fabric choices.

Resolution: the detail held by a digital image. The higher the resolution, the more detail an image carries. In digital imaging, resolution can be viewed as synonymous with pixel count.

Résumé: also known as curriculum vitae (CV). A résumé is a detailed formal overview of professional qualifications, experience, education, and accomplishments used in the job application process to demonstrate a candidate's abilities.

Sample: in the fashion field, this prototype garment or accessory is created in a designer's studio or sample room. For consistency and production pattern grading, every category uses its dedicated sample size. In the US, 4–6 is the dedicated sample size in women's clothing; 7–8 is the dedicated sample size in women's shoes. Depending on the geographic location, the sizing system may be different. Translation happens across sizing systems relative to market customs.

Sample room: this designer's work room is sometimes called an atelier (in haute couture houses) or studio (for independent designers). This is where sample garments are created. Typically, an assistant designer and sample maker may work with the designer in the sample room. The sample room is equipped with a draping form, cutting table, sewing machines, rolls of fabrics and trimmings, and all necessary tools and equipment.

Signature style: a visual statement demonstrating the essence of a designer's attitude and values within their designs.

Strategy: a plan of action designed to support the achievement of a goal. It takes into account value, messaging, and target audience.

Swatch board: an inspiration guide of fabric and color swatches used to explain the material quality of a collection as part of the design process.

Target audience: a group of consumers or customers predisposed to be interested in your product by specific factors such as age, location, or lifestyle.

Theme: a central concept used to build a strong core premise for the development of a fashion collection.

Trends: observation of styles, societal movements, and consumer behavior that can affect purchasing patterns and design development.

Typography: the style, shape, and visual character of letters used to express meaning.

Values: guiding principles that become fundamental beliefs dictating behavior as well as visual, verbal, and written expression for a person or an organization.

Vector: images in vector format are based upon mathematical equations rather than a solid colored square pixel. These images remain clean and smooth no matter how large or small the lines, curves, and points of an image become.

Voice: an extension of personal or signature style; a visual or verbal way of expressing a unique personal perspective.

Fabric terms

Batiste: a lightweight, sheer, plain weave fabric of mercerized cotton with a smooth, silky feel.

Brocade: a rich fabric woven with an elaborate embossed or embroidered surface effect, usually with different ground and pattern weaves featuring gold or silver thread.

Cashmere: fine, soft, and extremely warm, this is a luxurious and sustainable fiber obtained primarily from cashmere and pashmina goats.

Chiffon: a gossamer or gauze-like fabric of silk, rayon, or nylon. With a smooth feel and a transparent appearance, it is most commonly used in eveningwear, nightgowns, scarves, lingerie, and wedding dresses.

Cotton gauze (muslin): plain cotton fabric woven from evenly spun warps and wefts, or fillings. This fabric has a fine and smooth texture. It can be made in different weights. The lighter the weight, the higher the quality.

Indigo: a deep purplish-blue color. The indigo dye is obtained either from plant extraction (indigo plant) or created synthetically.

Jacquard weave: features an intricate pattern woven into the warp on a special mechanical loom. It is used in costly fabrics such as brocades, tapestries, and damasks.

Jersey: known for stretch, softness, and natural elasticity. It is a flat knit fabric originally made of wool, now also made of cotton or synthetic fibers.

Moiré: silk fabric that has been subjected to pressure rollers and heat to give it a reflective, rippled appearance.

Muslin: a loosely woven plain weave cotton fabric. Unbleached muslin is commonly used in garment design sample-making to test patterns.

Piqué: characterized by raised parallel cords or fine ribbing, which gives the material a subtle pattern and texture. It is durable, flexible, and breathes well.

Satin: a smooth, lustrous fabric with a complex weave that remains cool to the touch. Depending on whether you are a purist or not, it may be made of silk or synthetic materials.

Taffeta: a versatile lightweight fabric with a crisp texture and a subtle sheen. It may be made of natural or synthetic fibers. Body movement creates a characteristic rustle. Used in corsetry and evening wear, it holds its shape especially well.

Tweed: a rough woolen fabric. It is a classical menswear fabric of a soft, open, flexible texture in a plain weave with a twill or herringbone structure.

Index

Credits: a = above, b = below, m = middle, l = left, r = right

cover Courtesy Ikshit Pande. Quod S/S 2021. Photo by Walter Oro Abrahvo. Model: Tian-Yi Chang ; 4 Courtesy Queenie Qing Cao ; 7 La Moda CóModa illustrations, ©Agatha Ruiz de la Prada ; 9 Courtesy Minori Amada ; 13 Courtesy Katrin Schnabl. Photo by Danilo Hess. Model: Nina Vodopivech ; 16l ©Mark Mahaney ; 16m Photo: ©Bruno Staub. Model: Daniela Kocianova ; 16r Photo by Dia Dipasupil/Getty Images ; 16b Courtesy Stella McCartney ; 17l Lorado/Getty Images ; 17r Courtesy Allbirds ; 18 Pixelformula/Sipa/Shutterstock ; 19l dpa picture alliance/Alamy Stock Photo ; 19r © Anthea Simms ; 20 Photo by Jeff Spicer/BFC/Getty Images) ; 21 Pixelformula/Sipa/Shutterstock ; 22 Photo by Pierre Vauthey/Sygma/Sygma via Getty Images ; 23l © Yves Saint Laurent ; 23r © Yves Saint Laurent/© Droits réservés ; 24 Archive Gianfranco Ferré Foundation ; 25 Courtesy Anna Sui ; 39 Photos by Ugo Camara ; 28 Courtesy Emily Waters Lee ; 29 Courtesy Mayuri Sarof ; 30 Courtesy Céline Haddad ; 31 Courtesy Lishuang Xu ; 32 Courtesy Carla Amaning ; 33 Courtesy Amina Lyazidi ; 34-35 © T. Albu ; 36-37 Courtesy Mayuri Sarof ; 39 Courtesy Agatha Ruiz de la Prada ; 40-41al Courtesy Ikshit Pande. Photo by Pankaj Paul. Model: Tenzin Yonten ; 41ar Courtesy Ikshit Pande. Photo by Vikas Maurya assisted by Aayush Tuladhar. Model: Sakshi Bisht; 41b Courtesy Ikshit Pande ; 42 Photo by Victor VIRGILE/Gamma-Rapho/Getty Images ; 47 Archive Gianfranco Ferré Foundation ; 48 Courtesy Lamont O'Neal ; 49 Sebastian Tjsie ; 50 © Aurore de la Morinerie ; 51 © Antonio Soares ; 52 ©Dharti Patel; 53 Courtesy Lishuang Xu ; 54 © Stefan Radulescu ; 55 © Cem Bora ; 56-7 © T. Albu; 58-9 Courtesy Jesse Evans; 60-61 © T. Albu; 62-63 Courtesy Optitex; 64 Courtesy Ikshit Pande. Photo by Tommy Williams. Model: Owen Carr; 65-66 Courtesy Elena Moussa; 67 Courtesy Ikshit Pande. Photo by Vishal Chabbra. Model: Tenzin Chemi; 68-69 © T. Albu ; 71-73a Courtesy Djiun Wang ; 73b Courtesy Sebastian Tjsie ; 74 Courtesy Jingwen Xie ; 79 Courtesy Joan Dominique. Photo by M. Nahum-Albright ; 80 © Aurore de la Morinerie ; 85 Courtesy Mullenberg Designs ; 86 Getty Images; 88 Courtesy Mullenberg Designs; 89 Courtesy Pina Zangaro; 90a Courtesy Minori Amada; 90b Courtesy Louise Hidinger. Photo by Zhi Wei. Model: Milly Zhang ; 91a Courtesy Djiun Wang; 91b Courtesy Dyanna Csaposs; 92a Shutterstock; 92b Courtesy Coroflot; 93 Courtesy Katrin Schnabl. Photo by Matthew Reeves. Model: Kate Shannon; 95 Shutterstock/© T. Albu ; 96 Shutterstock/Courtesy Elena Moussa. Photo by Filippo Del Vita; 97 Courtesy Céline Haddad ; 101 Courtesy Dyanna Csaposs ; 102 Courtesy Queenie Qing Cao; 103a Courtesy Pauline Hilborn; 103b © T. Albu; 104 Courtesy Eleonora Gendler; 111al Photo by Victor Virgil/Getty Images; 111ar Photo by Pietro D'Aprano/Getty Images; 111b Photo by David Dee Delgado/Getty Images; 112a Photo Johnny Dufort/M+A Group112b Courtesy Viviane Sassen; 113 Courtesy Céline Haddad ; 114 Photo Sanjit Das/Bloomberg via Getty Images; 115 Dreamstime; 116 Alamy; 117 Shutterstock; 118l Courtesy Olga Singh; 118r Courtesy Céline Haddad. Photo by Roger Moukarzel ; 119 Seun Yeun Kim ; 121 Courtesy Man Yan. Photo by M. Nahum-Albright ; 122 Courtesy Mengao Xi. Photo by M. Nahum-Albright; 123 Courtesy Rich Daniel. Photo by M. Nahum-Albright; 128-29a Courtesy Céline Haddad. Photo by Roger Moukarzel. Model : Tati ; 129b Courtesy Céline Haddad. Photo by Roger Moukarzel. Model: Valeria; 131 Courtesy Céline Haddad ; 132 Céline Haddad. Photo by Roger Moukarzel. Videography by IMAXtree. Models : Tati and Joela ; 134 Courtesy Yuhan Bi. Photo by M. Nahum-Albright ; 141a Courtesy Ikshit Pande ; 141m Courtesy Olga Singh ; 141b Courtesy Joan Dominique ; 143a Courtesy Céline Haddad. Videography by IMAXtree. Model: Joela ; 143b Courtesy Ikshit Pande ; 145 Shutterstock ; 147 Shutterstock/Courtesy Stefan Radulescu. Model: Eliza Virban; 148a Courtesy Djiun Wang; 148b Courtesy; Selfridges; 149 © M. Nahum-Albright; 151 Getty Images; 152 Courtesy Agatha Agatha/Racoonandbabies. Photo by Vicky Tanzil; 157 Courtesy Jingwen Xie. Photo by Jingwen Xie. 158 Zinah Nur/Shutterstock; 159 Alina Sun/Shutterstock; 160al Courtesy Sara Cristina Vilasmil. Photo by Conrado Veliz. Model: Maya Touré. 160ar Photo by Edward Berthelot/Getty Images. 160bl Courtesy Ian C. Gonzalez. Photo by Ian C. Gonzales. Model: Audrey Wilkins. 160bm Courtesy Ikshit Pande. Special collaboration with GQ "The Expressionists". Model, styling, and makeup: Dame Imfala. 160br Courtesy Louise Hidinger. Photo by Zhi Wei. Model Ashley Mingot; 161 Shutterstock; 162 Courtesy of Belinda Jacobs of Techpacks.com; 163al Shutterstock; 163ar Courtesy Lectra; 163b Shutterstock; 164 © M. Nahum-Albright; 165 © T. Albu. Photo by T. Albu; 166 Courtesy Laurence King Publishing. Cover image: David Downton © 2004. Courtesy of The London College of Fashion. Cover design: Pentagram. Cover lettering: Marion Deuchars; 167 Shutterstock; 168 Courtesy Elena Moussa. Photo by Filippo Del Vita. Model: Axelle Mariani; 169 Courtesy Djiun Wang. Photo by Djiun Wang; 170 Photo by Elisabetta Villa/Getty Images; 171al Courtesy Mu-Tien Liu; 171ar Courtesy Alicia Mennen. Photo by Alicia Mennen. Model: Alicia Mennen; 171b Courtesy Céline Haddad. Photo by Roger Moukarzel. Model: Tati and Valeria ; 172l Courtesy Katrin Schnabl ; 172r Courtesy Katrin Schnabl. Photo by Cheryl Mann. Performers : Rory Hohenstein and Christine Rocas ; 173 Photo by Leon Neal/Getty Images; 174 Courtesy WGSN and Coloro; 176 Courtesy Emily Waters; 178al Courtesy Sebastian Tjsie. Photo by M. Nahum-Albright; 178ar Courtesy Chang Shao. Photo by M. Nahum-Albright; 178b 123RF; 179 Getty Images/© T. Albu; 181 Courtesy Lou Malta. Photo by M. Nahum-Albright; 182 Getty Images; 185al Céline Haddad. Photo by Roger Moukarzel ; Courtesy 185am Courtesy Agatha Agatha, Raccoonandbabies. Photo by Glenn Prasetya. Model: Nikita Philpott; 185ar Courtesy Hannah Dean; 185bl Courtesy Ikshit Pande. Photo by Rashmi Nair. Model: Amlanjyoti Bora; 185bm Courtesy Qing Guo; 185br Courtesy Olga Singh; 186a Courtesy Céline Haddad. Photo by Roger Moukarzel ; 187l Courtesy Céline Haddad. Photo by Roger Moukarzel. Models : Tati and Joela ; 187r Courtesy Céline Haddad. Photo by Roger Moukarzel. Model : Tati ; 188 Courtesy Agatha Agatha ; 189 Courtesy Agatha Agatha, Raccoonbabies. Photo by Glenn Prasetya. Model : Alexa Lourdy ; 190l Courtesy Hannah Dean. Photo by Alex Underwood; 190r Courtesy Hannah Dean. Models : Rufus Stewart and Al Gill ; 191 Courtesy Hannah Dean ; 192 Courtesy Ikshit Pande. Photo by Miguel Herrera ; 193 Courtesy Ikshit Pande. Model: Sakshi Bisht. Photo by Vishal Chabbra. Model : Tenzin Chemi ; 194-95 Courtesy Qing Guo ; 196 Courtesy Olga Singh ; 197l Courtesy Olga Singh. Photo by Olga Singh. Model : Karina Erzunova ; 197r Courtesy Olga Singh. Photo by Dasha Dare. Model : Nadia Okhunova; 199 © T. Albu.

Acknowledgments

This practical guide grew from our many conversations about the fashion landscape and the need for young designers to develop a clear unique voice. Years of teaching revealed the absence of a practical comprehensive guide addressing the use of strategy, personal branding, and social media to enter an evolving industry. We collaborated, each bringing complementary, professional strengths. The resulting book reaches well past the portfolio to speak more widely about concepts, images, and communication.

Long before the inception of this project, we routinely exchanged ideas on the topic. Our successful working relationship was always based on reciprocal respect and the ability to interweave our professional skills for student's educational benefit.

So, before we recognize the people who have been involved and supported this project, we want to acknowledge the true satisfaction we experienced by working together on this book.

We wish we had been able to include all the impressive material that was contributed, but this of course was not possible. With heartfelt thanks we acknowledge the generosity of all the students and colleagues past and present who contributed visual material and insights.

Thank you: Ikshit Pande, Agatha Agatha, Céline Haddad, Olga Singh, Hannah Dean and Qing Guo. We especially appreciate these young designers for candidly sharing their experiences, struggles and successes to benefit our readers.

With kind professionalism, insightful suggestions were offered by our editor, Sophie Wise, and the editorial team at Laurence King. We also want to thank Heather Vickers, picture researcher, and our book designer Lizzie Ballantyne. We could not have asked for better partners and thank them for their dedication to this project.

We are grateful to Agatha Ruiz de la Prada for her kind contributions and foreword. We admire her prolific work and bold, colorful spirit.

As we researched and organized, we were ably assisted by our loyal intern, Chao Shang. She was committed, and integral to our work, helping us at every turn, to move forward more swiftly, smoothly, and effectively.

Tamara's personal note:

Wholehearted enormous thanks to my parents for their unconditional affection and support, as they nurtured my love for the fashion artform. My gratitude to my brother Volodea, and my sister Vicky, for their patience and understanding. They put up with many rejected Skype calls – "Not now, I'm working with Michelle". Special thanks must go to my nephew Ted, and my niece Mira, who followed closely the lengthy progress of this project, and offered their advice.

An enormous thank to colleagues Larisa Iosilevich and Brigitte Conti for their generosity in recommending outstanding students to help us illustrate fashion subjects. I am indebted to the fashion and costume designer Professor Katrine Schnabl, for taking the time to select from her wide range of work and document it for us.

I deeply thank Pamela Trought Klein, my former chair, for fifteen wonderful years working together at Parsons School of Design. She provided the big break that began my teaching career by taking a chance on an emigrant artist/designer with a heavy accent. Her guidance and generosity during those first years was immeasurable.

Michelle's personal note:

During the development of this book, I often thought gratefully of Professor Charles Goslin, a mentor who long after his passing still guides me. While he taught me how to communicate visually in a beautiful and clear manner, he fostered a love of ideas as living visual entities. The process of writing this book allowed me the opportunity to appreciate the training graciously offered to me throughout my career by talented professional colleagues too numerous to name.

A big thank you to Christina Conception of Don Congdon Associates, who offered invaluable publishing information and guidance to two publishing novices.

I could not have dedicated myself to this endeavor without the support and forbearance of my husband Donn and daughter Elizabeth. They, and my sister, Joyce Fogel, were always there to cheer me on. Thank you to our favorite black cat, Noir, who consistently cuddled on my lap with encouragement and approval.

In the end, this book honors my parents, Clarice, and Gino Nahum, who taught me the value of education and the beauty of art. Their love and nurture made me the person and educator I am.